The Price They Paid

The Price They Paid

DESEGREGATION IN AN AFRICAN AMERICAN COMMUNITY

Vivian Gunn Morris
Curtis L. Morris

Foreword by Asa G. Hilliard, III

Teachers College
Columbia University
New York and London

Published by Teachers College Press, 1234 Amsterdam Avenue, New York, NY 10027

Library of Congress Cataloging-in-Publication Data

Morris, Vivian Gunn, 1941–
    The price they paid : desegregation in an African American community / Vivian Gunn Morris, Curtis L. Morris ; foreword by Asa G. Hilliard, III.
        p. cm.
    Includes bibliographical references (p.   ) and index.
    ISBN 0-8077-4235-X (pbk. : alk. paper) — ISBN 0-8077-4236-8 (cloth : alk. paper)
    1. African Americans—Education—Alabama—Tuscumbia—Case studies.
    2. School integration—Alabama—Tuscumbia—Case studies.   3. Tuscumbia (Ala.)—
    Race relations—Case studies.   I. Morris, Curtis L., 1940–   II. Title.

    LC2803.T85 M67 2002
    379.2'63'09761915—dc21   2002019431

ISBN 0-8077-4235-X (paper)
ISBN 0-8077-4236-8 (cloth)

Printed on acid-free paper

Manufactured in the United States of America

09 08 07 06 05 04 03 02   8 7 6 5 4 3 2 1

To our grandson,
James Curtis Green

Contents

Part II. School Life Before and After Desegregation

Foreword

THE PROBLEMS OF African people worldwide have a context and a reality that are not well understood, even by African people themselves. Matters of education and socialization are really aspects of the whole experience of African people.

In order to understand the situation now, we need a general comprehension of the continuity of the culture. African people have a history of thousands of years during which extremely sophisticated and effective systems of education were created (Hilliard, 1997). Some of these systems still exist on the continent (Griaule & Dieterlan, 1986). They have been studied by behavioral scientists and educators. In some cases these socialization systems have been imitated to such an extent that they have initiated fundamental changes in Western European systems of education and socialization (Pearce, 1977).

What is more interesting, however, is the extent to which Africans in America preserve the deep structure, the elements of our ancient African systems (Webber, 1978). Whenever we have the freedom to control the education and socialization process, the old values manifest themselves (Hilliard, 1997). These include a belief in genius in all of our children, the belief that the entire community is responsible for the education and socialization of every child, the belief in the efficacy of nurturing as an approach to instruction, the belief in the spiritual nature of the teaching and learning process, the belief in our place in the universe as a cosmic people who are reflections of the divine, respect for the environment, a hunger for the truth, and the belief in social responsibility, among others.

If African people could ever come to know the traditions in education and socialization from our core cultural base, we would be empowered beyond measure, simply because no other system seems to match the quality of what we have had before (Hilliard, 1997). Slavery, segregation, and White-supremacy ideology interrupted and had a major impact on the African community's control of the education and socialization process and on the ideas that are common to our community.

Our response to the MAAFA* (the terror of slavery, colonization, segregation, and White-supremacy ideology and behavior) can now be understood. At every turn we have grasped the opportunity, seized it, exploited every opening to create powerful educational and socialization experiences for children (Anderson, 1988).

In short, with few to no resources outside of ourselves, we have "made a way out of no way." We have created awesome results, even during the slave period, throughout the segregation period, up to the present time (Webber, 1978). These enormous achievements have been "under the radar," "invisible," even to our own community. It was not that way in the beginning.

Following the 1954 Supreme Court ruling in *Brown vs. Board of Education of Topeka, Kansas*, research done by Hamilton (2000) and reported in his classic article "Race and Education: A Search for Legitimacy" demonstrated clearly that the African American community, at that time, was demanding an education very different from what European Americans envisioned for us. African Americans had no doubts about their capacity to teach their children. What they wanted was their fair share of the resources for education in order to have a curriculum that was legitimate and culturally salient, and to have control of the education of their children. Neither segregation or "integration" got to the root of our problems. The evil system of segregation had to be destroyed. However, no remedy that destroys us as a family can be accepted. Racially "mixed" classes may not be a problem, but, they do not offer the way to our getting the highest quality of education. It is desirable but not sufficient to have experiences with all types of people. The demands of the African community were hijacked in the court system and among supporters who saw the solutions to our problems as the breakdown of communities by closing community institutions and sending children to be integrated into predominately White schools. We now have nearly 45 years of experience with this system, during which time whole city school systems were reshaped by White flight and even some Black flight from the public school systems that serve our children. There was also a phenomenal growth of special education and tracking. These are the "savage inequalities" that have been documented by Jonathan Kozol (1991). I have detailed some of these issues elsewhere (Hilliard, 1997).

---

*The term MAAFA is a Kiswahili word that means unimaginable disaster. It is not an acronym. It refers to our devastation, used to differentiate African slavery, colonization, and segregation/apartheid from a "holocaust." MAAFA was first introduced by Dr. Marimba Ani. It is now fairly widely accepted to describe our unique experiences.

All of this is to be seen as a preamble to my comments about this important work done by Morris and Morris, *The Price They Paid: Desegregation in an African American Community.* Although millions, even billions of dollars have been spent on educational research over the past century, many significant pieces of information have yet to become part of mainstream understanding. In fact, some research entities have suggested that the very process of doing research may not only obscure vital information, but contribute to the construction of damaging structures. In this environment, it is extremely important that work such as this done by the Morrises be expanded.

In this case study, the Morrises reveal the details and texture of school segregation and integration in one Alabama community. This outstanding account highlights the centrality of relationships in the design and implementation of powerful education settings. Teachers who were an integral part of the school community brought those relationships into their work at school. They clearly identified with the students and their families, and created an environment where children could have the widest range of experiences, and where parents and community were intimately involved in school matters (Ladson-Billings, 1994).

The Morrises speak of the "unmet promises of desegregation." I wonder if there were any real promises beyond body mixing. Desegregation promises never included the vital "ethic of caring." In fact, as the students' experiences document in this instance show, the children often didn't feel safe in their new environment, did not feel that it was their school, did not experience a sense of belonging in their new school. In fact, they often felt hostility, not only from students, but worse, from those who were in the position to teach and lead them. We learn something of the power of these schools from this case study. We also see how vital community institutions through which parents and community could shape their schools and their children were destroyed.

What is significant in this analysis is how straightforward the design for education can be. The actions of school leaders and teachers do not stand out because of complicated and intricate teaching methodologies or theories. They stand out because of the quality of human relationships and the unqualified commitment of educators to the welfare of their students and the community itself. Up until this very time, we have been unable to acknowledge the savage inequalities in our schools. If we were to focus our research on these inequalities, then their magnitude as the primary factors in the achievement gap would be grasped. We would then be in a position to understand and to take the necessary steps to change the situation in dramatic ways, perhaps by a return to what we know. Those principles can still be applied.

Morris and Morris, through their careful research, have painted a picture of reality, the type of picture that educators, community leaders, and policymakers must see in order to give a proper assessment of what is going on and what should be done.

This clear, straightforward presentation is as necessary as it is powerful. The Morrises' orientation to research should be imitated by others. Their analyses are worthy of the most serious consideration.

Asa G. Hilliard, III
Professor of Urban Education
Georgia State University
June 2001

Acknowledgments

OUR THANKS are extended to members of the Trenholm High School community, who shared a portion of their history with us by completing questionnaires and interviews and by sharing a variety of personal and professional documents that provided the data for these stories. We also acknowledge the special efforts of two colleagues, Lucindia Chance and Satomi Taylor, who read and gave feedback on the first draft of the manuscript.

Introduction

THIS BOOK, *The Price They Paid: Desegregation in an African American Community*, focuses on how selected lessons learned from the school stories of one small Northwest Alabama community are related to the unmet promises of school desegregation. What was it like in this legally segregated African American school during the 20th century from the perspective of students, teachers, administrators, parents, and the community? How did school life change during the first 15 years (from 1965 to 1980) in the desegregated school setting? What was gained? What was lost? What are the implications of these findings for schools in the 21st century?

In answering these questions, this volume builds on and extends stories and lessons learned in our previous book, *Creating Caring and Nurturing Educational Environments for African American Children* (Morris & Morris, 2000a). As we begin a new century of living, loving, learning and schooling, it seems important to reflect on the lessons of the past century so that we can build on our mutual strengths as well as avoid repeating the mistakes of the past.

Many reports about the impact of desegregation focus on broad statistics related to school closings, displacement of African American teachers and administrators, decreased involvement of families in school activities, and the increased rate of suspensions and expulsions of African Americans students. This book provides an inside view of what happened in one school community from the perspectives of the people who lived the experience—African American students, parents, teachers, and administrators.

This school community described what it meant to care for, nurture, educate, and protect their children from the ravages of racial segregation, as well as the negative impact of school desegregation in their community. As we researched the stories of other similar communities and the lives of African Americans who helped to change America, it appeared there was a common national goal, particularly in the first 70 years of the 20th century, that gave direction to African Americans in caring for and educating their children. As you read their stories, speeches, and letters you will find

1

that African Americans throughout the country perceived education as the primary means for pursuing the goal of "uplifting the race." Their strong belief in this goal united them to persist and to develop cooperative efforts, which enabled them to build effective school communities for their children despite separate and unequal treatment by the White establishment.

This is a retrospective look at what it meant for African Americans to live and learn in both the segregated African American school *and* the desegregated predominately White school in their community. It is important for teachers, administrators, parents, and policymakers to listen to these voices from the 20th century as we plan effective schooling for *all* children in 21st-century America.

As you read these selected stories (there are many more), you will find, as we did, that many of the questions and issues that we are presently grappling with in 21st-century education circles were clearly conceived, articulated, and dealt with by players in this small African American village, and others just like it, early in and throughout the 20th century. Why haven't we heard more of these stories before? Why do they not already permeate the history of education in our country?

For too long, American citizens were led to believe that the contributions of African Americans to education in this country were limited primarily to pioneers like Booker T. Washington and George Washington Carver, especially in the early days of the 20th century. Later, the leadership of Martin Luther King, Jr., was credited with gaining the rights of African Americans in a variety of areas, including education. Thus, most history of American education books contain but a few pages outlining very briefly the education of African Americans in this country, while the lion's share of education history is devoted to the contributions of European Americans and European philosophers and educators who influenced the ideals and structures of education in our country.

Much too often, separate African American schools were characterized as having poor teachers and administrators, poorly operated academic programs and activities, uncaring and neglectful parents, dilapidated school buildings, and scarce instructional resources. Legal desegregation of schools, ushered in by *Brown vs. Board of Education of Topeka, Kansas;* was viewed by many as the saving grace to rescue African American children from these perilous wilderness conditions and deliver them to the promised land of schooling where they sat next to White children who were already enrolled in schools in the land of Canaan, flowing with milk and honey and all the other good things Black students had missed for so many decades. There appeared to be no real need to dig deeper, to explore below the surface of what was happening internally in those separate African American buildings from the perspective of the school administrators and teachers, and the parents and students they served.

You may not recognize the names of these ordinary school administrators, teachers, parents, and students who worked together to build an extraordinary school community for African American children. But you will marvel at the ideals and the persistent efforts to provide effective segregated schooling for their children and at the way they view the future of effective schooling in desegregated schools in their community. In the process, you may even recognize similar stories from your own school community.

Undergraduate and graduate students enrolled in teacher education programs will want to read this book as they prepare to teach African American children and other children of color. College and university teacher educators and professors of educational administration and African and African American Studies programs will find this volume helpful as they extend their knowledge and that of their students about the history of African American education. Both scholars and practitioners in education, as well as parents, community leaders, and other laypeople, will find some useful insights that will guide them in planning and supporting quality education for all children in our country.

TRENHOLM HIGH SCHOOL COMMUNITY

Trenholm High School was a small African American school that operated in Tuscumbia, Alabama, for more than 90 years. It appears that the school had its beginning as the Osborne Academy in 1877 (Morris & Morris, 2000a). The authors of this book graduated from Trenholm High School in 1959. Established as an elementary school, Trenholm grew to become a 1–12 school by 1921. In 1969, the school building was closed and demolished and all African American children in grades 7–12 were assigned to attend the desegregated, formerly all-White school across town. At that time, elementary school buildings in Tuscumbia, though with only token desegregation, were located in both African American and White communities (Morris & Morris, 2000a).

Not only was the building destroyed, but most of the records documenting the long history of the school were destroyed as well. Trenholm High School served as the center for culture, recreation, leadership, and education for the African American community at a time when African Americans did not have access to other community resources, as did White citizens. Although few official records are available on graduation rates and state or national standardized tests, a large number of the graduates

from Trenholm pursued postsecondary education and launched successful careers in a variety of technical, skilled, and professional areas. A typi-
cal class was much like ours in 1959 with 19 students, where an estimated
75% or more of the class attended postsecondary institutions. And many
of the graduates, like us, were among the first generation in their families
to attend a college or university. Many of our parents did not complete high
school.

It was one of those small African American school communities of
which you might say "There must be something in the water," because so
many of its graduates were successful in their chosen careers and were
productive citizens in the local community and in communities across the
country. Why did so many African American students from this small
school community, with scant resources, do so well? Initially, it was our
charge to reconstruct this history for ourselves and for our community.
However, as we reviewed the related literature and looked at other studies about segregated and desegregated schooling of African Americans, we
discovered there was a wider audience that needed to hear this story (Morris & Morris, 2000a). We believe that an understanding of the impact of
both segregated and desegregated schooling in the lives of African American children and their communities will help us to understand what we
need in all communities from our schools.

William Mansel Long, Sr., was a 1924 graduate of Trenholm High
School, a parent, and a community activist in Tuscumbia until his death in
the late 1990s. He communicated the sentiment of many African Americans regarding segregation and desegregation of schools in that community, stating that

> the Supreme Court decision of 1954 didn't give us school integration in
> Tuscumbia; it gave us school elimination. It eliminated the Black school
> and forced the Black children to go to the White school. . . . The only
> thing [sic] we've ever had in our community is a church and a school.
> They have been vital influences in our way of life, and to take a church
> or school out of a community is like taking a hymnbook and a Bible [out
> of the church]. That's what happened to us [when the school was taken
> out of our community]. (Long, 1981, p. 203)

Harvard University sociologist Charles V. Willie agreed with Mr. Long's
conclusion regarding African Americans being the losers in the desegregation process:

> Whites took the concept of integration and hijacked it. Furthermore, they
> dropped the educational components that Blacks had assumed would
> go hand in hand with integration. It was like turning to the fox that had

been stealing the chickens and then saying, "Fox, develop a plan to secure the chicken house" (Hendrie, 2000, p. 72).

This book is based on a long-term research study entitled "The Education of African American Children in a Small Southern Town" that was
initiated in 1981. Several articles, reports, and presentations (Morris, 1993,
2000; Morris & Morris, 1981, 1993, 1995, 2000a, 2000b, 2002; Morris, Morris,
& Taylor, 1998) have been based on the data. The first book-length manuscript, *Creating Caring and Nurturing Educational Environments for African
American Children*, was published in 2000 (Morris & Morris, 2000a).

Most of the interview data on which this present book is based were
collected in 1998 and 1999. Four major research questions were addressed
in the larger study: What were the factors that the school community perceived as making their school a good school? What kinds of educational
experiences did teachers and principals view as important for the successful education of African American children? How did the school interact
with parents and the community? How did the educational environment
change when the segregated school was closed and African American children began attending the newly desegregated school?

In addition to the data provided in 34 interviews, the alumni (1924–
1980 graduates), teachers, administrators, and parents (119 former students
who attended Trenholm or Deshler, the desegregated high school from 1909
to 1980) completed a 27-item questionnaire that included their perceptions
of the quality of education in their school(s). Additional sources included
school board minutes, school yearbooks, local newspapers, student hand-
books, accreditation reports, and a variety of public and private documents.

African American children in Tuscumbia, Alabama, attended Trenholm
High School for most of the 20th century, from 1900 to 1969. Trenholm was
established as the second high school for African Americans in the state of
Alabama, after Parker High School in Birmingham. The high school department was initiated in 1896, the same year the *Plessy vs. Ferguson* Supreme
Court decision established "separate but equal" as the law of the land. While
the elementary grades had been started years earlier, the high school was
supported with money raised by the African American citizens. By 1910, the
school had grades 1–11 and grew to have its first 4-year graduating class
in 1922.

The curriculum at Trenholm incorporated primarily the philosophy
of W. E. B. Du Bois with classical or liberal studies rather than the Hampton-
Tuskegee industrial education model that was perfected by Booker T.
Washington at Tuskegee Institute, about 250 miles south of Tuscumbia. For
example, by 1910 the secondary curriculum included the following courses:
English, mathematics, Latin, German, pedagogy and psychology, physics,

biology, and history (Jones, 1969). For many years, African American students from other small towns and rural areas in North Alabama and Mississippi boarded with Tuscumbia families to pursue a high school diploma at Trenholm. While many elementary schools were established in nearby rural areas during the 1900–1935 time period, Anderson (1988) noted that high schools for African Americans were not available in many southern communities until after World War II.

By the time the Trenholm school building was closed by court order in 1969, the physical plant consisted of a brick veneer building, the main unit built in 1939, with 12 classrooms, a library, a science laboratory, a separate lunch room, a band room, home economics and auto mechanic shop facilities, and a long-awaited standard-size gymnasium that was completed in 1960.

For too many years, classrooms were overcrowded, the buildings were too hot or too cold, and there was too little equipment and supplies in the science lab and regular classrooms, and too few books in the library. We played baseball, basketball, football, ring games; practiced for field and track activities; and jumped roped on eroding red clay playgrounds where there was not enough equipment to accommodate the student enrollment. The building was notorious for the poorly functioning toilets in the boys' and girls' restrooms, which were shared with their teachers.

Yet despite the lack of financial resources to adequately maintain the physical plant and to purchase books, supplies, and equipment needed for the academic program, many students eagerly looked forward to attending their classes each day for 12 years of schooling. Students, parents, and community residents attribute this attitude to the caring and nurturing educational environment created by dedicated and committed teachers and principals.

Trenholm High School was located southeast of the Tuscumbia downtown area in the heart of the African American community. The school was located on a two-acre plot of land that was donated by African American citizens. At its height in the mid-1950s, the school had an estimated enrollment of 500 students. The majority of the teachers lived in a four- or five-block radius of the school building, as did more than 70% of the students.

It was no accident that the majority of the African American population in Tuscumbia settled in the southeastern part of the town. In 1906, less than one year after the Tuscumbia Colored Public School/Trenholm High School building was moved from the Deloney Hill to the site at 11th and High Streets, a notice was listed in the *American Star* advertising the availability of cheap land near the school building:

> Don't let the cheap lots near Friendship Hall escape your notice. Cluster your homes around your church, your school, your hall of fellowship, and especially near the home of your devoted and earnest principal and teacher, Prof. G. W. Trenholm. Make it a settlement that every one in Tuscumbia will be proud of. So see F. T. Gilmore about these lots at once. They are selling. ("Brief and Special Mention," 1906)

Based on the language used in the text (the repeated use of the word "your"), F. T. Gilmore was most likely a White realtor or owner of property in the southeastern section of the town.

In October of that same year (1906), Prof. H. E. Levi, associate editor of the *American Star* and principal of the North Alabama Baptist Academy at Courtland (a private academy for African American children in a nearby county), echoed the sentiments of F. T. Gilmore, urging African Americans to settle in the southeastern part of town for reasons in addition to the cost of the land:

> In securing homes care must be taken: First to purchase in a negro community for mutual protection and in school and church development; second, the moral conditions should be favorable to character building. In settling too much stress cannot be put upon the moral and the educational status of the locality. . . . The white man has set the pace, and we must follow or be forced to perpetual poverty and dependence. . . . Now is the opportune time to seek good homes in good negro settlements. ("Negro's Last," 1906)

It appears that the community was settled as suggested by Gilmore and Levi, as noted above. One Trenholm graduate, who lived in the African American community from the early 1940s through the early 1960s, noted the impact of the "Negro settlement":

> There was a real sense of community. I mean the school being the centerpiece of the small community, the small black community. And there were churches, four consecutive blocks there were churches. . . . So, everything kind of focused and circulated around that little area where we lived. And you felt connected to the people who were there, with the older people, younger people, generations of people that lived there. And the older people, always had a great affinity for them because of some of the stories they could tell . . . about the community and how it developed and about some old family member that we had just heard about. And so the stories that were told there were a sense of history. It happened there and how the people of the community came there to live and to call this their home. (Morris & Morris, 2000a)

By 1940, the majority of African American businesses in the town were located adjacent to the school on South Washington Street. The area was known in the community as "the block." Most of the students passed through this area going to and from school each day. For many decades, the businesses included the neighborhood barbershop, the poolroom, and two to three grocery stores where students purchased snacks and school supplies. The hall used by the Masons and the Eastern Stars was located there, as well as various adult night spots such as the Pussy Willow, the Dew Drop Inn, and the Paradise Inn. The funeral home for the community, Thompson and Son's, was (and still is) three blocks from the site of the school building. Two White-owned grocery stores were located for many years in the same block as the funeral home. It appeared that each of the stores had a large customer base in the African American community. Whenever there was a fund raiser at the school to purchase band uniforms or stage curtains or to finance a trip to Washington, D.C., for the senior class, these businesses were active participants in the process.

HISTORY OF THE TOWN OF TUSCUMBIA

Tuscumbia bears the name of the Chickasaw chief who lived in the area when white settlers arrived in 1815. Chief Tuscumbia is reported to have sold the land to Michael Dixon in 1815 for $5 and two poleaxes. The town was chartered in 1817 and incorporated as the first city in Northwest Alabama in 1820, just one year after Alabama became a state. Nestled in the extreme northwest section of the state next to Tennessee and Mississippi, Tuscumbia is located 145 miles east of Memphis, 115 miles southwest of Nashville, and 100 miles northwest of Birmingham. Tuscumbia is the county seat of Colbert County with a current population of 8,400 and is part of a quad-cities area that is often referred to as the Muscle Shoals area. It is also considered a part of the Florence Metropolitan area. Florence, with a population of 36,400, is the largest of the four cities; there is a total population of 136,900 in the metropolitan area. The Muscle Shoals area is rich in natural resources; the Tennessee River runs through it; and several local industries have contributed over the years to the economic development of the area including the Tennessee Valley Authority, Reynolds Metals Aluminum Company, Ford Motor Company, Union Carbide, and the Colbert Steam Plant. The University of North Alabama (formerly Florence State College) and Shoals Northwest Community College offer postsecondary educational opportunities for area residents (Board Minutes, 1955; Desegregation Plan, 1970; Leftwich, 1935; Shoals Life, 1998).

Tuscumbia is probably best known as the birthplace of Helen Keller, a deaf-blind woman who graduated from college and became a writer, an international lecturer, and a champion of those with disabilities. The annual Helen Keller festival is celebrated each year with a play, *The Miracle Worker*, staged on the grounds of her home, Ivy Green, along with other activities celebrating her achievements. A local hospital bears her name as does the first public library established in Alabama, located in her hometown. For many decades, Tuscumbia was the center of economic and industrial growth in Northwest Alabama and served as a political base for many state and local democrats (Leftwich, 1935; *Report of Visiting Committee*, 1955; Shoals Life, 1998). Former President Jimmy Carter chose this small town as the site to launch his unsuccessful 1980 presidential campaign.

SCHOOLS IN TUSCUMBIA

The town of Tuscumbia has generally maintained a fairly consistent population of 75% White and 25% African American. Having closed Trenholm High School in 1969, Tuscumbia City Schools currently operates a unitary school system with 1,490 students in four schools: (1) Deshler High School, grades 9–12; (2) Northside Middle, grades 6–8; (3) R. E. Thompson, grades 3–5; and (4) Southside Elementary, grades K–2. The district also operates an early childhood center in a former elementary school building.

It appears that former slaves in Tuscumbia and throughout the South emerged from the slave period with a strong desire to read and write and to control their own education. For them, literacy was a sign of freedom and liberation, something that had been denied them by law during the slave period (Anderson, 1988). Several schools were established by the Freedmen's Bureau and by various aid and missionary societies during Reconstruction. One of those schools was in Tuscumbia (Fleming, 1905). The first known recorded account of legal education for African Americans in Tuscumbia was in 1870 when the Freedman's Bureau school was taught by Judge (or Dr.) Wingo and his daughter "at the church at the foot of the Hill" and he reportedly gave a "general satisfaction to all interested," and faithfully discharged his duties (*Alabamian*, 1870). Leftwich (1935) also reported that Parson George Ricks, a former slave and preacher, donated land on which a frame structure was built that served as both church and schoolhouse during this period. In 1881, a Tuscumbia newspaper reported that there were some "colored schools" in the town (*Democrat*, 1881).

An 1878 newspaper article indicated that this town of 2,000 inhabitants had "seven churches, five white and two colored, two white female and one white male school and one colored" (Tuscumbia, 1878). The colored school mentioned was most likely the Osborne Academy, which probably became the Tuscumbia Colored Public School in 1887 and Trenholm High School in 1921. The Tuscumbia City Council formally allocated money for public schools in 1887 (*Weekly Dispatch*, 1887).

The Freedmen's Bureau school that operated in 1870 might have been conducted in the same church structure described by Leftwich (1935). Before becoming such a school, the school held in the church might have operated as a "Sabbath" school. Anderson (1988) reported that during this period many former slaves established Sabbath schools that operated evenings and weekends to provide literacy training for both children and adults. It appears that the school was later moved to a lot adjacent to the church building to be established as the Osborne Academy in 1877 and later named the Colored Public School in 1887. This seems likely because local newspaper accounts and county deed records affirm that the Osborne Academy was on the same tract of land as the Colored Public School. The Colored Public School was moved a few blocks south to the corner of 11th and High Streets, the site of Trenholm High School when it closed in 1969 ("Colbert County," 1881; "Colored City," 1905; Leftwich, 1935; *Tuscumbia Dispatch*, 1905). In Tuscumbia, as in other southern communities, African Americans donated land, school buildings, instructional resources, and equipment to local school boards controlled by Whites in order to receive monies allocated by the state to support public schools for their children (Anderson, 1988; Board Minutes, 1955).

Anderson (1988) reported that former slaves were among the first native southerners to campaign for universal state-supported public education. Du Bois had also stated this premise: "Public education for all at public expense was, in the South, a Negro idea" (quoted in Anderson, 1988, p. 6). While the former slaves willingly accepted assistance from northern missionary societies and the Freedmen's Bureau, they expressed the desire to control their education by establishing their own trustees or advisory boards, and hiring African American teachers and administrators (DuBois, 1989). And in other southern communities like Tuscumbia, African Americans were able to exercise a great deal of that control for many decades prior to the desegregation of schools in the mid-20th century.

AFRICAN AMERICANS' PERCEPTIONS OF SEGREGATED AND DESEGREGATED SCHOOLING IN TUSCUMBIA

Based on questionnaire and interview data from graduates of Trenholm High School and Deshler High School (from 1909 to 1980) and Trenholm attendees (those who attended Trenholm before it closed but graduated from Deshler, the desegregated high school), three major factors contributed to Trenholm's being a good school: qualified, dedicated and caring teachers; the range of school programs and activities; and parental and community support and involvement (Morris & Morris, 2000a). With desegregation, these three critical elements were eliminated or threatened in the lives of African American schoolchildren in Tuscumbia and other towns and cities throughout the country. These three elements are critical indicators of a quality school but are often less visible than standardized test scores, buildings, equipment, and instructional resources. Baking powder, by weight, is relatively unimportant in the baking of bread. However, bread without baking powder may give you an unfulfilled culinary experience. Likewise, luxurious buildings with all the latest technological resources and equipment but without teachers who care about and are committed to the children they teach can produce poor-quality educational experiences for the children—the intended beneficiaries of all the resources provided.

Tuscumbia City Schools did not implement a school desegregation plan (Freedom of Choice) until 1965, 11 years after the *Brown* Decision was issued by the Supreme Court in 1954. The school board adopted a desegregation plan only a few days after the government threatened to pull federal funds from the district. While there were no outward signs of problems associated with the desegregation of schools in Tuscumbia in September 1965, African American parents and students experienced a number of problems that interfered with the ability of students to focus on educational tasks. No one stood in the schoolhouse door to prevent the African American students from enrolling at the previously all-White schools or stood in front of the building to call them names. Nor were National Guard troops needed to ensure their safety. However, parents and students believed that racial discrimination was practiced by White students in their refusal to sit next to African American students in class and in the practice of "accidental/intentional" bumping and hitting in the hallways and in physical education classes, and by both teachers and students in the use of derogatory names.

African American parents felt that their children were punished unfairly and were discouraged from using their talents, and that parents and their children were treated with hostility. African American students felt that some teachers were insensitive in the manner in which they handled classroom topics related to the history and experiences of African Americans. They also felt that they had to prove their worth and their abilities while White students did not. And when they did, they were considered to be "unusual" or as one student said a "novelty" among their race. While these students were able to survive, they never felt that they "fitted in" or felt safe and secure as they had at Trenholm High School.

The African American students believed that to a great degree they no longer had the caring teachers who were present at Trenholm and they were restricted in their participation in extracurricular activities with the "new rules" at the desegregated high school. Parental and community support and involvement in the life of the school were hampered because the desegregated high school had several years earlier disbanded the PTA, an organization through which the African American community had exerted strong leadership in support of activities at Trenholm.

While all African American students enrolled in grades 7–12 began attending Deshler High School in fall 1969, elementary schools operating under the Freedom of Choice plan had achieved only token desegregation. No White children had chosen to enroll at the Southside Elementary School, which was built in the African American community in 1966 and had an enrollment of 210. Eighty-seven of the 542 students at Northside Elementary were African American, and three African American students were enrolled at R. E. Thompson Elementary (Desegregation Plan, 1970). Significant changes were made in the racial composition of Southside Elementary only when the school board decided that this school would be the location for all students enrolled in grades K–3 in the city. The district's desegregation report showed that by fall 1980, the enrollment of Southside Elementary was 60% White and 40% non-White, much closer to the racial composition of the city, which was 75% White, 25% non-White (Desegregation, n.d.).

OVERVIEW OF THE BOOK

The Price They Paid: Desegregation in an African American Community is organized into nine chapters. Part I, Chapters 1, 2, and 3, consists of a letter (written by Dr. William Hooper Councill) and two speeches (by George Washington Trenholm) written in the first two decades of the 20th century, which set the stage for segregated education in the local community and in the state of Alabama. Councill and Trenholm were outstanding African American educational leaders who influenced education in Tuscumbia, the state of Alabama, and beyond. These chapters reveal that these two educators were well informed, articulate, and astutely aware of the political and economic factors affecting the education of African Americans in the local community, the state, and the country as a whole. The documents included in these three chapters also clearly debunk the myths that perpetuated the idea of a lack of intelligence and capability in African American educators in the early 20th century. These two men were examples of African American educators in the South who worked with their communities to provide quality schooling for African American children despite the lack of adequate resources. They were men of both words and action and courageous risk-takers. Both Councill and Trenholm communicated the critical educational needs of their people at a time when African Americans in this country were lynched not only for noncriminal deeds, but because of a mere glance or phrase that Whites decided to take as an offense.

In Chapter 1, Dr. Councill, president of Alabama A & M Institute (now Alabama A & M University), addresses the White people of Alabama following the ratification of the state's sixth constitution in 1901. His letter communicates the plight of African American citizens in Alabama at the beginning of the 20th century, especially as related to the critical issues of education and voting rights. Dr. Councill's letter is included here because as a leading educator in North Alabama he had a great influence on the establishment and continuing development of schools and on teachers and administrators for African Americans in Tuscumbia and the surrounding area.

Chapter 2 contains the first of two speeches by George Washington Trenholm, the third principal of the Tuscumbia Colored Public School, named Trenholm High School in 1921. This first speech was delivered at the Alabama State Teachers' Association held in Selma, Alabama, in 1912. Mr. Trenholm was president of the association at the time of this speech. He addressed the status of African American education in Alabama and listed 12 major changes that needed to be made.

The speech in Chapter 3 was delivered at the meeting of the National Association of Teachers in Colored Schools (c. 1911). Mr. Trenholm emphasized the need for African Americans to focus their energies on developing public high schools in the South. He presented the model that had been successfully implemented in the community of Tuscumbia, Alabama, where he was principal.

Part II begins with Chapters 4 and 5, which provide a glimpse of what life was like inside this segregated African American school community, with a special focus on the leadership opportunities that were an integral part of what happened both inside and outside the school building for school-age children. Visits by outstanding African American leaders to the community were common experiences that stimulated students to aspire to careers in important technical, skilled, and professional areas. In Chapter 4, a 1945 graduate of Trenholm High School recounts her personal encounter with Dr. George Washington Carver, the famous scientist from Tuskegee Institute (now Tuskegee University) when he made a visit to the Muscle Shoals area in 1937 to deliver a speech at the first meeting of the Wilson Dam Section of the American Chemical Society. Since there were no hotels for African Americans in the area, Dr. Carver stayed in the home of an African American family in Tuscumbia.

In Chapter 5, several graduates of Trenholm High School communicate the way it felt to be students in a caring and nurturing educational environment that provided an atmosphere much like that of a family and how this affected them while students and later in their personal and professional lives. This chapter also reveals stories regarding the active involvement of parents and other community members in the life of school-age children, in the school building and in the community.

Chapter 6 focuses on the unmet promises of school desegregation. This chapter describes the expectations regarding desegregated schools as compared with the reality of what happened to African American students in the desegregated, predominately White high school in their town. African American students, teachers, and parents compare their experiences at both schools, and discuss both the losses and the gains at the desegregated school. The experiences of this African American school community are not unlike those of African American children throughout the South, as well as in other regions in our country.

In Chapter 7, a virus is used as a metaphor to demonstrate the profound negative impact of using skin color and race as a basis for preferential treatment of students in educational environments. This chapter addresses some events from primary grades through high school that took place in both the segregated African American school building and the desegregated school building prior to the closing of the Trenholm High School building in 1969.

Chapter 8 provides a glimpse of what life was like for African American students and their parents for the first 15 years of the desegregated high school, the formerly all-White school outside their community. In this chapter, titled "The Myth of the Unusual Negro," students relate how Whites (administrators, teachers, and students) expressed surprise or thought they (African American students) were a novelty or unusual among their race if they exhibited high academic skills or were able to address administrators, students, and teachers in articulate, intelligent ways.

In Chapter 9, the authors take a look at selected lessons about segregated and desegregated schooling learned from the school stories of this small Northwest Alabama community. This retrospective look at issues and concerns about the education of African American children is reflective of some of the same problems communities are grappling with throughout this nation. Some of the insights gained from this study can serve as a springboard for thinking about what we can do as a nation to provide a quality education for *all* of our children in the early decades of the 21st century.

PART ONE

Setting the Stage for a New Century: Councill and Trenholm

CHAPTER ONE

William Hooper Councill: Address to the White People of Alabama

THIS IS THE first of three chapters that communicate the state of segregated education in Tuscumbia and throughout Alabama during the early decades of the 20th century. This first chapter in Part I consists largely of the writings of Dr. William Hooper Councill, president of Alabama A & M Institute from 1875 to 1909. Beginning in the late 1880s, Dr. Councill made frequent visits to Tuscumbia and nearby towns. Professor Councill, an ex-slave, established the Huntsville Normal School (Alabama A & M) in 1875. He appeared to have had a great influence on the establishment and continuing development of schools and teachers for African Americans in Northwest Alabama. Seven years prior to the establishment of the Tuscumbia Colored Public School/Trenholm High School in 1887, Dr. Councill made a speech to a large audience at the county court house in Tuscumbia. One third of those in attendance were colored men (*Democrat*, 1880).

Mr. Councill conducted the summer institute for teachers in the county in 1889 (*North Alabamian*, 1889). In July 1896, a local newspaper reported that "Prof. W. H. Councill, President of the Colored Normal School near Huntsville, one of the ablest and most intellectual men of his race in Alabama and the South, was a visitor to Tuscumbia last Sunday. We like to meet a colored man like Prof Council" (*North Alabamian*, 1896). Mr. Councill spoke again at the courthouse in December 1896 at the invitation of G. W. Trenholm, principal of the Tuscumbia Colored Public School. G. W. Trenholm was mentored by Mr. Councill while a student at Alabama A & M. The *Weekly Dispatch* noted that "Professor Trenholm received his training under the well known Prof. W. H. Council at Huntsville, Alabama, one of the ablest educators in the South, and in a large measure his training has to do with his success as a teacher" (*Weekly Dispatch*, 1898). In 1901, Professor Councill spoke at the building of the Tuscumbia Colored Public School. A local newspaper reported that "a crowded house was present and his lecture was simply grand" (*Weekly Dispatch*, 1901).

The American Star gave this account of the commencement address delivered by Dr. Councill on May 15, 1902:

> He held his vast audience spell-bound for more than an hour, and when he had finished the people said that it seems that he had just been speaking for fifteen minutes. Dr. Councill's address was sound and practical, strong and logical, forcible and scholarly, eloquent and fascinating. He gave the people what they needed. He pointed out their weakness and showed clearly how the race could become powerful and useful. (City School, 1902)

Because of Mr. Councill's continuing involvement in area educational circles, it was not surprising that three of the four early principals at the Tuscumbia Colored Public Colored School—from 1889 to 1920—were graduates of the Alabama A & M Institute where Mr. Councill was president, namely, W. T. Breeding, G. W. Trenholm, and E. Z. Matthews. These three educators were probably recruited to the teacher training program at Alabama A & M, like many others, via one of the letters that President Councill used to recruit qualified students. An example of such a letter is in Morrison (1994, pp. 72–74):

> Normal, Ala.
> June 15, 1897
>
> Mr. Dear Young Friend:
>   Have you ever thought very seriously about improving your condition? Have you ever thought seriously about making your muscles more valuable by mixing more brains with them? You can be dignified, intelligent, industrious young man, if you so desire. All good people wish young men well, and willingly give them a strong, hearty push up the hill of life. But after all, every young man must make himself. People like to honor an intelligent, upright, industrious young man, but an ignorant, idle, vicious, impolite man is shunned by all good men. What are you striving to be, my young friend? Are you at work? Are you educating yourself, or helping parents, or educating a sister, or buying a home? Are you spending your money and time to no profit? Be a man. The race needs you. The country needs you. Do you know that brains are the most valuable investment you can make? There are so many chances for you to become educated. While all of our great schools are willing to help you, still you are able, by saving your money, to pay your way through school, and have all your time to study and learn a good trade. Too many of our young men throw away their money

and they try to work their way through school. Often this is a tedious process, and they become discouraged and fall out. Save your money and pay your own way. This is far better. If, after you have done all in your power, and you find yourself without money, you will find our school willing to give you brains for your muscle. But at all hazards, be a man or die trying. Do not delay another hour. Start now. What can you do for yourself? We want strong young men—we want cultivated brains and trained muscles to build up the Negro race. The A & M College, Normal, Alabama, desires to help you to be all that God intends you to be. So stand up my young friend, and be a man. God helps those who help themselves. Write to me.

Your friend,
W. H. Councill

It's evident that both his speeches and his letters were very persuasive.

The state of Alabama ratified its sixth constitution in 1901. This new constitution went into effect on Thanksgiving Day, Thursday, November 28, 1901 (*American Star*, 1901c). It appears that a great deal of the debate prior to the voters' approval of the new constitution centered on the rights of the Negro population to vote and to receive a separate, equal education. G. W. Trenholm wrote several articles in the *American Star* about W. H. Councill's efforts to influence the members of the constitutional convention regarding education in particular. In May 1901, Mr. Trenholm wrote:

> Dr. W. H. Councill, president of the A. and M. College, has addressed an able letter in behalf of negro education to the constitutional convention which is now in session at Montgomery, Ala. Prof. Councill never fails to put in a manly plea for his race whenever he can. He deserves the thanks of the entire race. (*American Star*, 1901a)

Also, the Colbert County Teachers' Institute, of which G. W. Trenholm was the conductor, sent the following resolution to the constitutional convention in June 1901:

> We, the colored teachers of Colbert county assembled in Tuscumbia in Institute, after cool and deliberate consideration, knowing that the constitutional convention now in session in Montgomery, Ala., is discussing the advisability of the disfranchisement of the negroes in the state, and whereas there is a strong feeling favoring the elimination of the negro vote, Resolved that we disapprove of any such legislation as would indicate discrimination between the races. Resolved further, that we favor an educational qualification irrespective of race. (*American Star*, 1901b)

In the December 12, 1901, issue of the *American Star*, G. W. Trenholm reported that Professor Councill had addressed a letter to the White people of Alabama regarding the new Alabama constitution. He stated:

> Prof. W. H. Councill, Ph. D., addressed an able, thoughtful and manly letter to the white people of Alabama on November 28th in reference to the new constitution. It was indeed a manly plea in behalf of the colored people. Prof. Councill is one of the strongest, best men of the race. He is ever found pleading for his race whom he so dearly loves. We feel confident that this address will redound to the good of all Alabama, white and colored. (*American Star*, 1901d).

At the beginning of the 20th century, W. E. B. Du Bois (1903/1989), in his seminal work, *The Souls of Black Folk*, declared that the problem of the 20th century was "the problem of the color line." He said that

> the problem of the twentieth century is the problem of the color-line— the relation of the darker to the lighter races of men in Asia and Africa, in America and the islands of the sea. It was a phase of this problem that caused the Civil War; and however much they who marched South and North in 1861 may have fixed on the technical points of union and local autonomy as a shibboleth, all nevertheless knew, as we know, that the question of Negro slavery was the real cause of the conflict. Curious it was, too, how this deeper question ever forced itself to the surface despite effort and disclaimer. (p. 14)

Du Bois (1903/1989) and other scholars, such as Woodson (1933/1992) and later Anderson (1988), shed further light on the "rightful place" of African Americans in the South and the kind of education that was demanded by northern philanthropists and southern White planters in order to maintain the southern way of life. In the early decades of the 20th century, northern philanthropists and southern White planters used terms like *thriftless, careless, shiftless,* and *idle by disposition* to describe African American adults as a rationale for denying them universal public-supported education, the right to vote, and economic security as a free people. They suggested that African Americans were inferior and childlike. If they were to be educated at all, they needed industrial education to prepare themselves for their "rightful place" in their environment as farm workers and domestics. Southern Whites believed that "when they [African Americans] learn to spell dog and cat they throw away the hoe" (Anderson, 1988, p. 97). And then, who would do the backbreaking work at menial wages that was the major source of wealth of the agricultural South and fueled the economy of the industrial North?

Woodson (1933/1992) also noted the negative characteristics that had been attributed to African Americans by many White citizens. He stated that an African American was "pictured as a human being of the lower order, unable to subject passion to reason, and therefore useful only when made the hewer of wood and the drawer of water for others" (p. 21). Anderson (1988) claimed that "many white landowners opposed black schooling on economic grounds because they believed that reading, writing, and arithmetic would make black workers discontented with unskilled and semiskilled farm labor" (p. 96). Some White southerners suggested that schools for African Americans were dangerous because they created hotbeds of arrogance and aggression, and tended to make African Americans idle and vicious and enabled them to compete with Whites. Furthermore, when African Americans insisted on establishing classical liberal courses of study in their schools, they were hungry for prestige and merely "imitating Whites" or "acting White" (Anderson, 1988).

Du Bois (1903/1989) agreed with the southern planters that "an educated Negro *was* [emphasis added] a dangerous Negro." He further stated that "the South was not wholly wrong: for education among all kinds of men always has had, and always will have, an element of danger and revolution, of dissatisfaction and discontent. Nevertheless, men strive to know" (p. 28).

In this 1901 letter to the White people of Alabama, Councill attempted to convince Whites that the educated Negro was not the criminal Negro, as was communicated in the campaign to ratify the state constitution of 1901—a campaign to deny the vote and equal access to education to African Americans. He used their own data to demonstrate that the majority of African Americans who could read and write continued to serve Whites in unskilled and semiskilled jobs, and that only a small percentage of literate African Americans were imprisoned or engaged in teaching, preaching, and other professional work. It appeared to be very important for Whites to be assured that African Americans were not being educated for jobs in which they might be in competition with Whites or "imitating Whites."

Councill's letter began with a reminder of his loyalty and service to the White people of Alabama for more than 50 years, both as a slave and as a free man.

> I have served you in slavery and in freedom for over half a century. I have stood with you for "good government" for a quarter of a century. As all of past life has been devoted to your service and to the welfare of my race, I believe that you will grant me a hearing now.

I love Alabama. I have been true to her at home and abroad. I have never breathed one word against her. I have all along trusted her white people. I revere the names of her long lines of noble sons with untarnished honor, who scorned wrong and hate injustice. Their faith in right gave birth to your Confederate monument which stands on Capitol Hill representing what they regarded as truth. But today, I am alarmed! I tremble for the future of my people in Alabama, unless you come to our rescue. The recent campaign was one of bitterness and abuse of my people. Many of the public speakers did not appeal to the highest sentiment in man, but held up the Negro in a manner to make the white masses hostile to him. With all your best efforts for many years to come, it will be hard to undo the harm which was done to my race by that campaign into which was put so much unkind feeling. Not that you put a premium on suffrage. That was right. Not that the white man become supreme in government. He was that already. But in the sentiment manufactured against us. Was such a campaign necessary? There could have been but one result—ratification—though the press and speakers had held their peace. Then why abuse and mortify the men who are trying hard to please you and serve you every hour? Do not misunderstand me. For God's sake do not misrepresent me. I have never asked for unqualified suffrage. Since a majority of the better elements of the white people of Alabama wanted the new constitution and promised better things under it, I was not against it. I am opposed to every phase of social equality so distasteful to us both, and in my opinion, detrimental to Southern society. There is no necessity for it. Ninety-nine thousand, nine hundred and ninety-nine (99,999) Negroes in every one hundred thousand (100,000) do not seek social equality, and if every Negro in the State sought it, it would not be. You know all this. Still we were abused, and the hostility of the lower element of your race aroused against us, while a quarter of a million of us were bowed, uncomplaining, at your cook pots, ironing boards, wash tubs, in your cotton fields, and in all the varied industries, loyal and true to you. We are in your hands as babes in the hands of giants, making no laws, construing no laws, executing no laws, holding no offices, composing no juries, forming no militia, a weak, powerless people, and still men acted toward us as if we had been Caesar's Legions in their palmiest days. If we were the strong and you were the weak, would not you be alarmed? I beg you in the name of your mothers who were cradled in the arms of black women, in the name of your fathers who were loved and served by our fathers, and in the name of the sacred dead in gray, around whose sad hearths we kept faithful vigil, to rise up and checkmate these evil influences which you have set on foot against us. You do not know the harm you have done. We know it. We feel it keenly in a hundred ways. Do not say that it is only the educated Negro who is disturbed. God grant that it were so. But the cut has entered the soul of the ignorant Negro whose benighted mind cannot gather light from the philosophy of history and strength from a knowledge of the ultimate triumph of right; but the stolid, sullenly silent man whom you must change into the citizen of hope and obedience, or drive into the stupid, hopeless, riotous creature of despair—a beast, a constant menace to be cured by the gatling gun.

Council emphasized that he was not requesting unqualified voting rights for Negroes or social equality for his people because this would be distasteful and detrimental to the Southern way of life. He noted that Whites were strong and Negroes were powerless ("as babes in the hands of giants"). So why then would some Whites stir up animosity and hostility toward his people—to do them harm? The *Plessy vs. Ferguson* decision of "separate but equal" was handed down just 5 years prior to Councill's letter, but as he pointed out, it appeared that the new constitution would allow unequal spending for schools for Negro children.

In the next section of his letter, Councill also skillfully and subtly communicated that the economic security of the South was really built on the backs of slaves and former slaves, as did Woodson (1933/1992) and later Anderson (1988). He pointed out that African Americans were part of the productive population in the state, both in what they said and in what they did.

The new constitution makes it possible for the darkest wrong to be perpetrated on Negro education and many of the campaign speakers and writers prepared the public to commit this wrong. You can compel a Negro school to run ten months on one hundred dollars and appropriate one thousand dollars for ten months to a white school under your new constitution. You must surely know that such injustice would not only drive away from you the loyal hearts of your Negro population, but would drive them from Alabama. Your own Dr. Curry told your Legislature that the Negro was, in certain counties, often defrauded out of his part of school funds under the old constitution. Who will guarantee that it will not be done to a greater extent under the new constitution? You got a new constitution, you said, to avoid the necessity of committing fraud in elections. You promised us righteous treatment in educational affairs. Your own statesmen say that the Negro pays taxes and still some men persist in saying that he does not. If you wish a division of the school funds on racial lines, go to the very bottom of the matter, and see who pulls the tax money from the bosom of the earth, the only original source of wealth. We do four-fifths of your agricultural labor and add four-fifths to your wealth from that source. Your own record shows that the mass of your Negro labor is not only law abiding but industrious. The proportion of Negro wage-earners to the entire Negro population in Alabama is greater than in any other Southern State except Louisiana. Give us our portion in equity and we will not complain. You promised to do this. You said that with the political matter settled, all else should be fair. I still have faith in you. Though you slay me, yet will I trust you. Present the question fairly to the popular vote of the white people of Alabama alone, I believe they would vote for a division of the school fund on the basis of scholastic enumeration, and they would enumerate fairly, too. Take this matter out of the hands of men who do not like my race. Let it rest on the Golden Rule, then peace, prosperity, and happiness will come to all our people, and your waste places will bloom. Leave it with men who hate us, who appeal to prejudice, and it will soon take the place of the political question just settled.

It is said that the educated Negro is the criminal Negro. We are in your fields, kitchens and shops at work. We cannot answer. But what are the facts as recorded by you in your books? Three million (3,000,000) Negroes can read and write. Only eleven thousand (11,000) Negroes who can read and write are in all the prisons of the country. Just one Negro in every hundred who can read and write is engaged in teaching, preaching, and other professional work. That is what your records tell. Does this show that the educated Negro is the criminal Negro, that all educated Negroes go into the professions and that education unfits the Negro for labor? Two million, nine hundred and fifty thousand (2,950,000) Negroes who can read and write are working every day for you in all grades of labor. Are not our virtues minimized and our sins magnified by men who do not like us? I do not hesitate to state as a fact that nine in every ten Negro teachers and preachers are loyal and true to the South, and hold up the best lights before the ignorant masses of the Negroes. Whether you accept it or not, these Negro teachers and preachers will be the life preservers among your laboring population in our state in less than fifty years.

We are part of your productive population. Please study us. Please look into what we are doing, and what we are teaching and preaching. I beg you not to listen to those who use our weakness to arouse prejudices to elevate them to position. We want only what is right. The better element of white people do not know what unnecessary insults and hardships are put upon we Negroes. We bear these things because we know that even a manly and most humble protest is often put down as impudence and arrogance. Nearly everywhere we turn, in cities, in backwoods—the Negro stands muzzled and manacled, and unkind white men belabor our backs with impunity. White men of Alabama, for God's sake look at this picture! It is not overdrawn. See the truth as it is before God and angels! Are you not debauching your own sons by lodging such privileges, and unholy power in the pigment of a man's skin? Punish the Negro—whip him until the blood runs in streams when he is wrong, but let justice be done him though the heavens fall— justice everywhere. Truth, Mercy and Justice will strengthen and adorn your race when it stands before the judgment bar of future intelligence and righteousness.

Councill appealed to the Whites' belief in a higher power in his letter. He pleaded to the "good White men" of Alabama to apply the Golden Rule; to use truth, mercy, and justice to their benefit at the final judgment in their relationships with African Americans. In the next section of his letter, he also appealed to the pride of the Whites of Alabama. Many southerners, both African American and White, believed that Georgia and Mississippi were always at the bottom of the heap in the United States as related to economic development, education, and racial relations—even below Alabama. So the White people of Alabama certainly did not want to be accused of being less fair (or more backward) than those of their adjacent sister states.

Mississippi disfranchised the Negro, but she is fair in education. Mississippi, the home of Jefferson Davis. Georgia stands up for Negro education. Georgia, the home of Alexander Stephens [vicepresident of the confederate states]! Mississippi welcomes the Negro to her borders. Texas gives princely support to Negro education and invites him to her territory. Can you see the signs of the times? Must your labor element be kept suspicious, treated wrong by the men who take advantage of the color of their skin— men who know the power in white and the weakness in black—or will you protect us and make life profitable and happy to us?

The Jewish people are examples of the triumph of right. Their history shows forth God's mercies in the life of people. It is a warning to cruel men. Every nation which has been cruel to the Jew is dead or dying. The Jew has served many nations for thousands of years. He was obedient to the laws of all, and bent his back to the stripes laid on by all. At last God has brought him to a land where he has peace and where those who once despised him honor him.

I have been loyal and true to you. I would be disloyal and untrue now if I did not speak. We love you, honor you and want to serve you. Encourage us. We need it.

I have presented conditions that cannot be cured by abuse, or general denial. I have presented conditions known to well informed people. I have presented conditions which you must strike down, or which will harm us all. I appeal to you—not to the north—not to Congress. They are powerless. You are all-powerful in this matter. I believe that you have the righteousness to correct these conditions and I trust it all in your hands.

If your race is in superior condition, then God has placed the races in inferior conditions under your care for kind treatment, and not to be mistreated and crushed. Will you do the work of God, or must He take it in His own hands as He has always done when men failed? The weak and unfortunate are His tenderest care.

"Right forever on the scaffold,
Wrong forever on the throne;
Yet that scaffold sways the future,
For behind the dim unknown
Standeth God within the shadow
Keeping watch above His own."

W. H. Councill
Normal, Alabama, November 28th, 1901 (Councill, 1901).

It appears that many of the statements made by Councill in this letter were designed to gain the resources that were needed for the education of African American citizens in the state of Alabama and to protect them from those Whites who would do them harm. He appealed to the pride and stated religious beliefs of Whites who were in power in the state. It is very likely that Councill, like many other African American educational leaders at the beginning of the 20th century, communicated what they believed that Whites in power wanted to hear about African Americans in order to receive the few resources that they did—rather than stating what they *really* believed and receive nothing.

For example, Anderson reported that most African Americans believed that the long-range purpose of education was "the intellectual and moral development of a responsible leadership class that would organize the masses and lead them to freedom and equality" (1988, p. 31). Thus, many African Americans who established elementary, secondary, and normal schools and institutions of higher education adopted the classical liberal curriculum to meet the goal of "uplifting the race." The development of leadership skills among students was an essential component of school experience. Yet those southern African American educators who persisted in adopting classical liberal courses of study were often denied financial support for their institutions by many northern philanthropic organizations while southern school officials who were intent on perpetuating the Hampton-Tuskegee industrial education model at all levels of schooling for African Americans were granted resources (Anderson, 1988).

Councill exerted considerable influence in the development of the classical secondary program at Trenholm High School despite the fact that many Whites believed that this model was exclusively for them. Councill exerted this influence through mentoring the principals and conducting professional-development activities for the faculty. Despite the appeals of educational leaders like Councill, the pattern of "separate and unequal" support of schools for segregated African American schools or schools with a majority of African American children and other children of color continued in Tuscumbia and in many other school systems throughout Alabama and the nation before and following the 1954 *Brown* decision.

CHAPTER TWO

Status of Negro Education in Alabama: Actions to Take

THE 1912 SPEECH by G. W. Trenholm reprinted in this chapter, combined with a second speech in Chapter 3 and Councill's letter in Chapter 1, provides a view of the developing system of public education in Alabama during the early decades of the 20th century. Twenty-four-year-old George Washington Trenholm was elected the third principal of the Tuscumbia Colored Public School (named Trenholm High School in 1921) on August 14, 1896. Three months earlier, on May 18, 1896, the Supreme Court had issued its *Plessy vs. Ferguson* decision, making "separate but equal" the law of the land.

Trenholm was born into a family of 11 children in Pineville, Shelby County, Alabama, to parents who were ex-slaves, Dan Trenholm and Mariah Doakes Walker. He married Ellen Brown in 1899, a graduate of the Tuscumbia Colored Public School and a teacher at the school when he arrived in Tuscumbia. Their only child, Harper Council Trenholm, was born in Tuscumbia in 1900. G. W. Trenholm's early education was in rural Shelby County schools. He spent 2 years at Marion Institute, and in 1894 he was awarded a diploma from the Normal Course of the American Correspondence Normal of Dansville, New York. After graduating as valedictorian of his class from Alabama A & M Institute in 1896, he continued his education while principal in Tuscumbia. In 1899, the Fenton (Michigan) Normal and Commercial College conferred on him the degree of Ph.B. (Bachelor of Philosophy). Beginning in 1906, he spent six summers of regular study at the University of Chicago, was awarded an honorary M.S. from Alabama in 1900 and two honorary degrees from Selma University, an A.M. (Masters of Arts) in 1915 and LL.D. (Doctor of Laws) in 1923 (Memorial Tribute, 1950; Memorial Tribute, 1957; Sheeler, 1945; Thompson, 1925).

G. W. Trenholm was principal of the Tuscumbia Colored Public School for 19½ years, from September 1896 to January 1, 1916, longer than any other principal before or since. Records also reveal that his tenure at Tuscumbia was the longest period of time that he spent in any of the professional positions (19 ½ years of his 32–year career) he held before his death on August 3, 1925. He left Tuscumbia in January 1916 to accept the full-time position of State Conductor or Supervisor of Teachers' Institutes (Memorial Tribute, 1950; Memorial Tribute, 1957; Sheeler, 1945; Thompson, 1925).

G. W. Trenholm presented the speech that follows at the Alabama State Teachers' Association meeting held at Selma, Alabama, on April 4, 1912. He was secretary of the association from 1900 to 1906, and president from 1910 to 1912, while principal of the Tuscumbia Colored Public School.

It is rather ironic that educational leaders at the end of the 20th century (and at the beginning of the 21st century) addressed almost exactly the same issues that Trenholm did in this 1912 speech. One of the issues that he emphasized several times in this presentation was the importance of the continuing professional development of teachers as the means for improving the educational achievement of students. He communicated the need for African American teachers to organize and collaborate in order to improve their teaching.

Trenholm divided his speech into four major parts. In the first section of this speech, he noted that even though this was a period of growth for the common school in the South, few African American children were enrolled in any school, public, private, or denominational. Trenholm described several other circumstances that prevailed throughout the 20th century in segregated African American schools and in "desegregated schools" where the majority of students were African American or other children of color: inequities in financial support, poor physical plants, teacher shortages, high teacher-student ratios, and overcrowded classrooms. Other factors Trenholm noted were high percentage of uncertified teachers, high percentage of teachers employed to teach outside their field of certification, inequities in teacher salaries, and teacher salaries lower than in careers that require much less education or training.

You could change the date to the late 20th century or early 21st century and you would find current educational leaders speaking about the same issues at our learned national societies or associations. In reading Trenholm's speech, perhaps the question that comes immediately to mind is: What has really changed?

Fellow teachers: It is indeed a great pleasure to come face to face and to be able to touch hands and exchange ideas with my faithful co-workers in Alabama for a wider, better, more general education and a nobler civilization.

Thoughtful and progressive Negro teachers everywhere fully realize that we, as well as teachers of the white race, need to get together, consult each other, plan and labor for the best interest and progress of our people in education.

It is self-evident that, each and every one standing alone, no class of workers can do their best and achieve the highest degree of success. In all walks of life, this fact is becoming more keenly realized. If persons who manufacture, construct and operate along material lines find it important and necessary to organize and work as one, how much more important and necessary must it be for teachers who are largely responsible for training and preparing men and women in character and efficiency—yea, in ability—for the successful operation of every worthy endeavor?

That Education Is Important and Necessary, No One Will Deny

It is the child's natural right. His minimum stock in learning should not fall below a common-school education. We can not well afford to deny his unquestioned right to receive all the education that our elementary schools can give. We cannot afford to neglect him, for when we do we trifle with precious soul-stuff.

Every observant student of man well knows that ignorance is a curse, be it voluntary or involuntary. Its record through all the ages is sufficient evidence. Truly has it been said: "Ignorance, added to the handicap of color, is too fearful a load with which to burden a child." In the long run, education is much cheaper than ignorance. School houses cost much less than jails. Teachers and educators are cheaper than judges and other court officials.

The education of the Negro youth of Alabama should claim the thoughtful attention and serious consideration of every thinking person in the State. The large majority of our children are growing up in absolute ignorance. They are not reached by our elementary schools. The public schools are falling short of their mission—the imparting of a primary education to the masses of the common people. It's a sad but true statement. Hence, we are brought face to face with a serious condition and a weighty problem.

Alabama's total school population is 712,769. Of this number 322,707 are Negro children. Last year only 156,761, or about 49 percent, were enrolled in our public, private and denominational schools. The average attendance was 90,000 or 57½ percent of the total enrollment and about 28 percent of the Negro school population. It is thus seen that about three-fourths of our children were practically out of school last year—"unreached by the powerful 'three-r' curriculum of the Common School." Last year 302,671, or 78 percent of the 390,062 white children in the State were enrolled in all the schools for their race.

During the past year $2,865,254 was expended in the maintenance of the common public schools. Of this amount the schools for the white children received, $2,507,669, while those for the Negro children received only $357,585. While the white school population is only 1.2 times that of the Negro, the common public schools for white children received seven times as much public money for their support as the same class of schools for the Negro. The average amount expended last year per Negro child was about $1.10, while the average amount expended per white child was about $6.43. State Superintendent Willingham, in discussing the amount expended in the maintenance of common schools, says: "It is fair to say that the money appropriated to them as public funds either by the State or by local taxation, the individual supplement paid by them being a much smaller proportion of the whole than that which obtained with respect to the schools for white children."

While the supplement paid for each Negro child is much smaller than that paid for each white child, it would be surprising to know just how much of the $357,585 expended for Negro education was really paid as a supplement by the Negro. He has certainly paid more of it than his best white friends realize. For Instance, the supplement paid by the Negro last year at Tuscumbia was $942.00; at Decatur, $287.50; at Tuscaloosa, 922.80; and at Demopolis, $240.40. The supplement at Tuscumbia was considerably more than $942.00, but I have given the amount which was included in the $347,585 reported by State Superintendent Willingham as having been expended on the Negro common schools. What the four small cities just mentioned did last year in the way of supplement for Negro Education is a fair example of what many other towns and cities did throughout Alabama.

For the year ending September 10, 1910, $329,094.83 was expended on common schools for the Negro and $2,417,378.57 on the common schools for white children. The Negroes paid as a supplement that year $31,235.30, while the white people paid $224,907.02. In other words, the supplement paid by the Negroes was about 9.5 percent of the whole amount expended on their schools, while the supplement paid by white people was about 9.3 percent of the whole amount expended on the schools for them.

The Teaching Force in This State Is Entirely Too Small

We need at least three times as many as we have. Alabama employed last year 6,836 white teachers and 2,384 colored. There was one white teacher employed to every 57 of the white school population and one Negro teacher to every 135 of the Negro school population.

If one competent teacher cannot successfully teach 57 children, how can one third-Grade Negro teacher teach 135? The record shows that more than two-thirds of the Negro teachers employed are on the Third-Grade register. The great majority of these have had practically no training in the Science of Education and the Art of Teaching.

Of the 2,384 Negro teachers employed in Alabama, 126, or 5.2 percent, hold Life Certificates; 48, or 2 percent, hold First-Grade; 608, or 25.5 percent, hold Second-Grade; and 1,602, or 67.2 percent, hold Third-Grade Certificates.

Fifteen years ago [1897], when the Negro population of Alabama was about 43,000 less than it is to-day, our teaching force in the public, private and denominational schools was about 2,400, about 200 of them being in the private and denominational schools. While the number of public school teachers has remained practically the same, there has been an increase of 125 percent in the teaching force of the private and denominational schools. There are in these schools to-day about 450 teachers. These schools now enroll about 10,000 students, against 4,000 fifteen years ago. The increase of students was 125 percent. Adding to the 2,384 teachers in the public schools the 450 in the other schools of the State, the grand total of teachers for the Negro is about 2,834.

The average salary during the past year for white teachers was $413 for the males and $350 for the females, while that for the Negro teachers was only $169 for the men and $150 for the women. We can not hope to get the best grade of teachers for this small salary. As a general rule, poor salary means poor teacher. "As is the teacher, so is the school." The State Superintendent of Education well says that "The Negro teachers, with an income of $169 and $150 respectively by men and women receive really less than is being paid to inferior men and women of that race who are employed as teamsters, washerwomen and cooks. Negroes thus employed usually get their board in addition to a larger annual cash income than is paid to Negro men and women who board themselves while teaching the Negro Youth."

In the third section of his presentation, Trenholm stated that there was no real commitment to a high school education for African American children at public expense. Also, there were different requirements for graduating high school in African American schools than in White high schools. He also pointed out the inequities in the training of teachers at the two land-grant institutions in the state, Alabama A & M for African Americans and Auburn for White teachers.

There Are Practically No Negro Public
High Schools in Alabama

The remarkable and praiseworthy movement during the past few years to establish county high schools has not even touched the Negro. Including the District Agricultural Schools, there are about 200 public high schools in the State for the education of white children. There are, according to the recent report of the United Commissioner of Education, four for the Negro. Added to this very small number there are a few grammar schools that give their pupils a year's training in high school studies after the completion of the prescribed elementary course.

In the white public schools last year there were enrolled 11,500 students, or about 3 percent of the white public school population and about 4 percent of the total enrollment. In the Negro public schools there were enrolled in high-school classes 468 pupils, or about 14 percent of the Negro school population and about 3 percent of the total enrollment. About 450 white teachers devoted practically all their time to the instruction of pupils in high schools, while not more than 40 percent of the 23 teachers, instructing Negro high-school students, devoted all their time to that grade of work. Practically none of the Negro public high schools require the same studies, for graduation, as is required by the white public high schools for a diploma.

The high-school situation for Negro education is more serious than that of the common school. The State feels that it ought to do something toward imparting a primary education to the Negro youth. There seems to be little or no public sentiment favoring high-school education for any percent of Negroes at public expense. The outlook is by no means encouraging.

President Williams of the National Association of Teachers in Colored Schools, says: "If Negroes are to have any leaders of considerable intelligence for the masses of their people who are being pushed farther and farther out of contact with the white people every day, they, too, must have a considerable number of high schools maintained at public expense. Social and economical conditions among the colored people themselves demand them. And the very pressure of the elementary schools makes high schools a necessity, not only for the sake of preparing efficient teachers for the elementary schools, but also to give a fitting outlet for the budding intelligence awakened in the lower schools."

What reasons can be given why we should not have a larger number of public high schools in this State? Why should not these high schools do for the Negro students what the white public high schools are doing for their pupils? In addition to the industrial courses (and too much praise can not be given to that line of education), why should not our State Normal Schools do for the prospective Negro teachers what the white State Normal Schools are doing for their prospective teachers? Why should not our State A. and M. College do for the Negro what is being done at Auburn for the white people? And why should not the private and denominational secondary schools and colleges for the Negro do for him just what the same class of schools for the whites are doing for their race? Why should our high-grade institutions content themselves in giving us only Second and Third-Grade teachers? Only three First-Grade Certificates were issued to Negro teachers in Alabama last year, while 318 were issued to white educators. During the same period 97 Life Certificates were issued to white teachers and not one was issued to the Negro. Can not, and will not, our normal schools and colleges change this condition?

In the next section of his presentation, Trenholm addressed a subject he described as being "unpopular to speak about": higher education for the Negro. He, like Du Bois (1903/1989), believed that a considerable number of African Americans must receive high-level training in order to develop the leadership and content skills required to educate the masses. He believed that African American leaders and teachers required the same kind of liberal education as Whites in order to carry out the quality work needed in secondary and normal schools.

*There Is Entirely Too Little Attention Given
to College Education in Alabama for the Negro*

In making this statement I am not unmindful of the fact that it is a little unpopular to speak out for the higher education of the

Negro. Neither am I unconscious of the fact that we must educate the masses of the Negro in the fundamental principles of a common-school course; develop their instinct of truth and justice, implanted in their hearts by the Almighty, and give them such industrial efficiency that they will make them such a factor in our industrial problems, that they can not be cancelled without serious detriment to the labor situation of our common country. If we do this for the masses we must have a considerable number of high-grade leaders, such as our high grade institutions are capable of producing.

During the past year there were 2,641 students in all the college departments of all the white colleges—public, private and denominational—in Alabama, while in all the college departments of all the Negro college in the State there were only 66 students, and three-fourths of these were in one college—Talladega. In other words, there was one pupil in college to every 147 of the white school population and only one student in college in every 4,889 of the Negro school population.

We can no more get along without the college than can the white race. We must have leaders and teachers of high ideals and liberal education; for without such our secondary and normal schools can not do the best work.

If we hope to succeed in America a considerable number of our boys and girls must be trained in the arts, sciences and professions. A one-sided education is a dangerous thing for any people. The Negro needs a full-rounded education. "Schools of every branch and every character are needed to make him a full-rounded man."

The race that neglects the college destroys the high school, and with the passing of the high school there can be no very great number of real first-class elementary schools to impart a primary education to the "common masses of the common people."

The majority of our schools are taught in churches and society halls. Worse than poor are the most of our rural school houses. In many of our towns and cities the same wretched conditions obtain. Dr. Dillard, of the Jeanes Fund, after making extensive visits in parts of the South, including our own State, writes: "With rare exceptions I found wretched conditions in the way of school houses and school equipments." In most of our cities the Negro school houses are badly overcrowded. Nothing more needs to be said regarding the general condition of Negro school houses in Alabama; for you, my fellow teachers, face the situation daily and you know too well the wretched conditions which obtain.

The facts and figures given in this discourse speak for themselves. What, now, can we do towards enlarging our educational forces? Can we not inaugurate some movement for the rescue of our children from the terrible estate of ignorance toward which they are steadily and rapidly marching? It is evident that much needs to be done if the education of our children is to be given anything of the impetus already given to the education of the children of the white race in Alabama. A noted educator has well said: "We must strive to win our boys and girls from ignorance as we are striving to win them from hell. We must build school houses for them as well as churches. We must support the teachers as well as the ministers—co-workers together in the same field. It is our divinely imposed duty to do both."

At the conclusion of his address, Trenholm made specific recommendations to improve the education of African Americans in Alabama. His list of recommendations is very similar to those articulated in 21st century publications or heard at conferences.

How shall we change the status of Negro education in Alabama?

1. *By improving our methods.* "The surest way," says Superintendent J. H. Phillips, "for teachers, principals and superintendents to improve their methods is to improve themselves." This proposition needs no argument—it is self-evident.
2. *By urging legislation for the improvement of our schools.* "Ask, and it shall be given you," says the Master. We ask for entirely too little. We need a strong committee to put our case before the Legislature. County High Schools having been given to whites, surely we can get a few district High Schools, if we ask for them in the right way.
3. *By helpful publication—turning on the light.* This Association should collect and publish from time to time data covering the material contributions that the Negroes are making towards their own education. "It seems to me, "says Mr. W. T. B. Williams, "to be clearly our duty, and the duty, too, of local educational associations, to learn the actual, specific homely and even unwelcome truth about colored school conditions and to make public this information. We should do this not for the sake of complaining nor in the spirit of bitterness, but for the sake of truth, which ought to arouse the colored people to overcome their own indifference and to secure to them the helpful interest of all those who are ever ready to help those who help themselves."

4. *By building more and better school houses.* By building more and better school houses, thoroughly equipping the same, so that both teacher and pupils may do their work under the most favorable conditions. Let us make use of the State fund set aside for that purpose. On October 1, 1911, the State had on hand for building and repairing school houses $83,029.63. On April 1, $67,000 was added to that amount, making a total of $150,029.63. On April 1, every year this amount will be increased by $67,000. We ought to use as much of this amount as possible. The people will rally to us if we will rally to them. If we point the way, they will follow. We can build school houses. In too many cases we are not disposed to build. "We as teachers are too willing to enter upon the fruits of another man's labors, and to teach in a hall or a church."

5. *By supplementing more substantially the public school fund and lengthening the school term.* "Any competent, wide-awake teacher can arouse sufficient interest in himself and his work to secure the active co-operation of the people not only in building, but also in supplementing." Several teachers have done so quite successfully, and what they have done and are now doing, others can do. Let the people be thoroughly and persistently aroused and they will take care of their schools in a substantial way.

6. *By co-operating with local public school boards.* We must reach the public school authority in our respective communities in the interest of better schools and more ample facilities for our schools. We must be aroused to a keener appreciation of the value of public education. We should give far greater attention toward making the work of the public school stronger and broader. We can not afford to show indifference, for we have too much at stake.

7. *By improving our private and denominational schools.* We do not need to establish any more of these; but we ought to give better support to those already in existence. We must rely more and more on the public schools to impart a primary education to the masses, as do the whites. While many of our private schools have done a great work and are still doing commendable work, we must not lose sight of the fact that they can never take the place nor do the work of the public school.

8. *By establishing high school departments in many of our well organized grammar schools in the larger towns and cities.* This can easily be done by organization and cooperation. This offers a splendid field for self-help. Let us meet the public school board, do as much as they, and get more public high schools going.

9. *By urging a considerable number of our brightest high-school graduates to enter college*, and thus fit themselves for larger usefulness.
10. *By laying a little more stress on real college work* in our institutions that are prepared to do that grade of work. I do not ask that we start any more colleges in Alabama: but I do urge that more college work be done, more attention be given to that grade of education—in our colleges now in existence. We can not afford to neglect so important a branch of education.
11. *By enriching our courses of study.* This may be done by the addition of some industries. This can be done in most, if not all, of our schools.
12. *By remaining in the community long enough to do some real good as a teacher.* Very little first-class work can be done in any place if it is to have a new teacher every session. Many of us have entirely too much of this spirit of moving every year into a new community.

Many other ways might be suggested for the improvement of our educational status, but I must conclude.

And now, fellow teachers, I have spoken to you along this line in hope that these remarks may induce a train of thought that will find expression in a concert of action looking forward toward a speedy and general improvement of our educational condition. We can not afford to stand passively by and see this great army of Negro children unreached by the wholesome influence of education. If we rest content while quite 200,000 of our youth go marching steadily into ignorance and consequent crime, we shall receive the great condemnation.

May we have the current and the wisdom to do our whole duty before it is too late. For truly has it been well said: "If man is to reach the highest state of happiness and usefulness, as well as to contribute his greatest possible service to mankind; if the community is to be moral and religious; if there is to be a high sense of intellectual and social responsibility; if pure living, noble ideals, honest enterprise and the advancement of civilization are to be encouraged and fostered, there must be a sound and correct educational sentiment. We must raise the standard of intelligence and morality through universal education."

Many of the inequities that existed at the beginning of the 20th century at Trenholm High School and other segregated schools for African Americans throughout Alabama and the South continued during the segregation period that ended in most communities by 1969. The inequities in

funding resulted in poor physical plants and inadequate instructional resources and equipment. School board minutes and other records showed
continuing inequities in salaries paid to African American teachers and
administrators for the first half of the century (Board minutes, 1907, 1944,
1950). Many African American men from Tuscumbia who earned college
degrees in teaching and returned home to live chose to work in local plants,
which did not require a college degree, because they could earn substantially higher salaries than teachers.

The Trenholm school community responded to many of the recommendations made during and after G. W. Trenholm's tenure as principal.
In 1922, Trenholm High School had its first group of students graduate with
4 years of high school, the first such group in North Alabama for African
American students and the second in the state. Professional-development
activities for teachers to improve their teaching methods were often conducted for school personnel in Tuscumbia and in neighboring towns under
the leadership of principals and teachers from Trenholm High School.

Trenholm High School had a fairly stable faculty. While some faculty
members remained in the community for only a few years, others spent
their entire teaching careers in Tuscumbia. Many of the teachers who had
a long tenure at the school were graduates of Trenholm High School who
went back home to teach after graduating primarily from the two state
normal schools, Alabama A & M and Alabama State. Thus, many of the
teachers did indeed "remain in the community long enough to do some
real good as a teacher."

As recommended by Mr. Trenholm, the African American community
worked cooperatively with the local school board through its Colored
Auxiliary Board, Citizen's Committee, and later the PTA to support the
educational needs of children in their community. However, after desegregation, it was very clear to the entire African American community that
the educational resources that had been provided for their children for more
than 90 years, even with all their efforts, were never "separate but equal."

The inequities in funding that existed in the elementary and high schools
were also evident at the historically Black colleges and universities (HBCUs)
in Alabama and in neighboring southern states where the majority of the
teachers of African American children were trained. These inequities continued to persist throughout the 20th century, before and following the
desegregation of public schools and colleges. Instead of fully funding teacher-
training institutions like Alabama A & M and Alabama State, authorities
established White state universities a few miles away in the same communities. In a few short years these new institutions had physical plants, instructional resources and equipment, and salaries that were far superior to those
at the HBCUs that were established decades earlier.

CHAPTER THREE

Concentration on Public High Schools in the South: What We Are Doing in Tuscumbia

IN THIS second speech, delivered in St. Louis at the National Association of Teachers in Colored Schools (c., 1911), George Washington Trenholm outlined his beliefs about developing public high schools for African Americans in the South. This speech, along with the one presented in Chapter 2 and Councill's letter in Chapter 1, comprises the historical framework for segregated schooling in the local community and in the state. The community education model that Trenholm recommended was already in place in the little town of Tuscumbia, Alabama, where he was principal of the Tuscumbia Colored Public School, later named Trenholm High School in his honor.

In the first part of his presentation, he urged his associates at the conference to focus their efforts on developing public high schools in the South rather than increasing the number of private secondary schools in their communities. He offered several reasons for this rationale: (1) common schools for Africans (and Whites) are a fixture that will receive increasing public support; (2) too few public high schools for African Americans have been established; (3) because of the poor financial support for private and denominational schools for African Americans, they cannot provide quality high-school-level work; and (4) Whites have abandoned their efforts to establish new private schools because state officals will provide more substantial support for public high schools. He stated:

> I appreciate the compliment of being accorded a place on today's program. The opportunity to speak to the National Association of Teachers in Colored Schools is a privilege and an honor that any one might keenly appreciate.
>
> I have been asked to speak on "Concentration on Public High Schools in the South Rather than Multiplying Private Secondary

Schools." This I will try to do in a plain simple way; for I shall make no attempt at eloquence nor rhetorical beauty.

Since all the States of the South support, in a measure, common schools for the Negro, it must be conceded that these schools are a fixture. From year to year the fund for their maintenance increases. Increasing attention is being given to their supervision. Better prepared teachers are being employed. Teachers are constantly reminded that *there must be some growing or there shall be some going.* So far as I know, white and colored teachers have to pass the same examinations and measure up to the same standard. If the South did not believe in good common schools for the Negro, the colored teacher would not be required to pass the same examination that the white teacher passes. What is true of examination requirements is equally true of attendance upon State Teachers' Institutes. The same law that compels the white teacher to attend an institute, forces the colored teacher to do likewise.

Since our common schools are a fixture, and will receive better support as the years come and go, would it not be well for us to give more attention to the creation of public high schools in the South? There are entirely too few Negro public high schools. The situation is rather alarming. According to the 1910 report of the U.S. Commissioner of Education, there were 141 Negro public high schools in the entire country. Of this number, Texas leads with 36; Missouri follows with 21; Georgia comes next with 11; Mississippi has 8; Tennessee and Kentucky have 7, each; Arkansas, Indiana, and Florida, 6 each; the Virginias, 5 each; Alabama, Illinois, and South Carolina, 4 each; Oklahoma has 3; Ohio, 2; Delaware, District of Columbia, Kansas, Louisiana, Maryland, and Pennsylvania have 1 each. Very few of these 141 Negro public high schools are taught in strictly high school buildings. The large majority are high school departments conducted in the same buildings with the elementary schools.

Of the 141 Negro public high schools in the United States, 124 are in the sixteen former slave States including the District of Columbia. The Negro school population between the ages of 5 and 18 for 1910 in these sixteen States and the District of Columbia was 3,038,710. Hence, there is but one public high school for every 24,505 of the Negro population. For the white people in the same year there were 10,072 public high schools. The white school population between the ages of 5 and 18 was 21,202,101; or one public school for every 2,105 of the white population. There were 41,194 teachers in the white public high schools against 473 in the

Negro public high schools, and 903,425 white students against 12,636 Negro students. Of these 12,636 Negro students, 8,251 were in distinct Negro high schools and 4,385 were in mixed or white high schools.

In the light of these facts, the question arises "How can 24,505 Negro boys and girls be educated in one poorly equipped public high school, when one fairly well equipped public high school cannot educate 2,105 white children?

The number of public high schools for the Negro must be increased. Some of our private and denominational schools have done good work in giving high school advantages to the Negro. Our white friends in the North and South have contributed liberally and constantly to the support of these schools. They are still doing so. But as these schools have been multiplied so very rapidly, it is rather difficult for them to live and do the best grade of work, for the simple reason that their financial support is too meagre. Then, too, these private secondary schools can no more take the place of the public high school for the Negro than they can for the white people. The white people have long since discontinued the founding of private secondary schools. Instead they are co-operating with public or State officials in the creation of public high schools, fully realizing that the State will support these schools more substantially from year to year. We should do likewise and get more public high schools going.

In the next section of his speech, Mr. Trenholm began to elaborate on the model for increasing the number of public high schools in the South for African American children that was in place in Tuscumbia. He suggested that the money that might be used to support a private school should be used to create a high school department at an already established elementary school. He also suggested that each community organize an auxiliary school board of African American citizens and an educational association whose members help to the meet needs of the school. The monies collected would then be used to pay the salaries of high school teachers. All of these efforts would be implemented in cooperation with the public school board.

One of the questions posed by Mr. Trenholm was of particular interest to the authors: "For who knows that by such co-operation the time will soon come in the South when there will be some Negro representative on many of the *regular* [emphasis added] public school boards?" The time did come in Tuscumbia when an African American citizen was named to the regular school board, but not until 63 years later. In 1972, James H. Floyd, a native of Tuscumbia who completed the elementary grades at Trenholm, was appointed to the board. At that time, Mr. Floyd was Director of Pupil Personnel Services for Florence City Schools in a neighboring town just six miles away. He was the only educator on the board; the other members were White businessmen. Based on the history of past actions of the local board of education, it was most likely that Mr. Floyd was appointed to the board because of coercion, rather than the cooperation Mr. Trenholm had proposed in his speech in 1911. For example, the school board did not adopt a plan to desegregate its schools until 1965, 11 years after the *Brown* decision, but only *12 days* after the passage of the Elementary and Secondary Education Act of 1965 (Morris & Morris, 2000a). Tuscumbia City Schools would have been ineligible to receive millions of dollars of federal funds provided under this new act if they had continued to operate segregated schools in the district (Yarbrough, 1981).

This pattern of appointing African American educators or African Americans who worked directly with children to the school board in Tuscumbia continued to the end of the 20th century. Mr. Floyd's appointment was followed by the appointments of Dr. Sim O. Harris and Ann P. Mullins. Both were employed by Florence City Schools. Mr. Trenholm continued his speech by saying:

> In every town or city where there is a good elementary school, we should co-operate with the school officials and establish a high school department rather than create a private secondary school. Let the money that we spend to support the private school go to maintain the high school department. This can be easily done. It is being done successfully in Tuscumbia, Alabama.
>
> If we can get together, organize a board of trustees, employ and pay two or three teachers to run a private school, why can we not concentrate our efforts on the public school, thereby strengthening poorly equipped elementary schools and adding to their curricula some high school branches? Where we support two or more weak teachers to run a private school, we can very easily employ and pay one or two strong, well qualified educators to do high school work in connection with the work done in our elementary schools. As a general rule, white school officials will welcome such a scheme of cooperation, and will do, in most cases, as much for the mainte-nance of the Negro public high school as the colored people them-selves, and will give better support to the elementary school. From year to year the white people will give more attention, better supervision, co-operation, and liberal financial support to these high schools until, eventually, they will support them entirely from

the public fund. This they will never do for the private secondary schools.

In every city and town in the South where there is no public high school for the Negro, there should be organized an auxiliary school board of nine, twelve, or fifteen public spirited members. The board should be made up of substantial citizens who represent the different religious denominations and secret societies. This auxiliary board should be the nucleus of an educational association of the city and town. The educational association might admit into its membership any person who agrees to contribute regularly to the educational interest of the city. The auxiliary school board should, in the beginning, be divided into three classes, so that a third of the members will serve one year, a third two years, and a third three years. Such a board would be continuous, having always a majority of experienced members. The educational association should elect or re-elect a third of the auxiliary board in every annual meeting of the association. The principal of the public school should be *ex-officio* member of the auxiliary school board. This board should employ the teacher or teachers for the high school department, become responsible for their salaries, and co-operate with the public school board in the general management of the school. The principal of the public school should be given the privilege to nominate the teachers to be elected by the auxiliary board. If the auxiliary board does its best and then fails to realize sufficient funds through the educational association to meet its obligation, the white school board would, in most cases, make up the deficit, if there be hearty co-operation on the part of the two boards. Then, too, the education and experience which the auxiliary board would get by contact and co-operation with the regular public school board would mean *far more* to the race in general and the auxiliary board in particular than can come to the Negro thru colored boards managing private secondary schools. For who knows that by such co-operation the time will not soon come in the South when there will be some Negro representative on many of the regular public school boards? The Negro can certainly lose nothing by such a scheme of co-operation.

The multiplication of private and denominational Negro high schools should be discouraged. For several reasons this should be done. First—They are giving our people a misconception of the place and work of the high school. They are not adequately supported nor well supervised. They can never take the place of the public high school; for they can never receive any or much support from the public school fund. Second—In many places they spring up in opposition to, and seek to destroy the usefulness of the public school. We need all our public schools and even many more. If we continue to establish these private secondary schools our educational system should be improved rather than crippled. The great majority of the so-called private secondary schools do but little or no real high school work. They are largely elementary schools. Every public school has a little endowment. The private school, in most cases, has none. Why, then, destroy the endowed school to run a school with practically no financial backing? Third—They cause public officials to fail to discharge their duty. In many places, except in large cities, the public schools are very poorly supported where these private secondary schools exist. In some towns there are practically no public schools for the Negro where these private schools are in operation. The white people say in action, let these private schools educate the Negro and let us use the public school fund to better equip our own schools. In other places school officials give the private institution a small appropriation annually, and thereby excuse themselves from the responsibility of maintaining Negro public schools. Fourth—Our present private and denominational schools and colleges are too poorly supported. They are all suffering and crying for better and more systematic financial backing. Pretty nearly every religious denomination has more schools than it can properly support, or does fully support. Then why should the number be increased? I do not plead for the destruction of any of our present private and denominational schools; for many of them have done well. The Mission Schools run in the interest of Negro education by our white friends of the North have done, and are still doing a great work. Too much can not be said in praise of the good work done and being done by these schools. Our white friends are not multiplying these Mission Schools, but are increasing their efficiency. They see to it that competent Christian teachers are employed. This can not be said of the many private schools that the Negro is now establishing; for in too many cases anybody, prepared or unprepared, is allowed to run a school for our people. We must discourage this practice, and let our motto be "No more private secondary schools, but more substantial support for such schools and colleges as now exist." Fifth—The white people, who surpass us in education, are not multiplying their number of private secondary schools. Long since they have ceased doing so. They have stressed the importance of the public high school to that extent that nearly all the larger towns and cities have good high schools. They are co-operating with State and school officials and getting county high schools established everywhere. They are giving the land, erecting suitable buildings, equipping the same, and paying a nice matriculation fee, in order that the States may take these county high schools and support them. The white people in Alabama, during the past two years, donated to the State in lands, buildings, and equipments, more than five hundred thousand dollars ($500,000) raised through private subscription, so that the number of county high schools might be increased. Should this not be a lesson to the Negro? Is it not a splendid example? And would it not be well for him to co-operate with school officials and get more and better public high schools established?

In this last section of his presentation, Mr. Trenholm provided some very specific details on how the high school department was created and maintained in Tuscumbia. The major source of funds was the "fifth Sunday rallies." Every month in which there was a fifth Sunday, the three principal African American churches in the community would take up a collection that would be given to the African American auxiliary school board to support needs at the school. The monies were used to pay the salaries of those high school teachers, who often also taught elementary classes before 2:00 P.M. These monies were also used to build buildings, to purchase equipment (e.g., the first piano for the school), and to purchase other essential instructional resources for the students. Very often, the auxiliary board and the community were required to raise money for special projects before the public school board would allocate public money (Morris & Morris, 2000a).

Anderson (1988) called this practice "double taxation." He stated:

> Since the end of the Reconstruction era black southerners had adapted to a structure of oppressive education by practicing double taxation. They had no choice but to pay both direct and indirect taxes for public education. Southern public school authorities diverted school taxes largely to the development of white public education. Blacks then resorted to making private contributions to finance public schools. To have their privately financed schools recognized and even partially supported by state and local school authorities, black southerners had to deed to the state their contributions of money, land and school equipment. (p. 156)

Anderson (1988) reported that many African American communities organized similar efforts to raise monies to build and support their schools. For example, in Hobson City, Alabama, the all-Black town organized an estimated 150 children into a "Snuff Box Brigade." By collecting pennies, nickels, and dimes in snuffboxes, the children raised more than $200 by the end of their first fund-raising rally. Fund-raising efforts like these continued until the school was closed in 1969.

> Lastly, what I have suggested in regard to co-operation with school officials has been, and is being done in Tuscumbia, Alabama. There we have a splendid auxiliary school board of fifteen public spirited men and an active educational association. Hearty co-operation with the public school officials has greatly strengthened our elementary school work and has given us a high school department. The auxiliary board pays the salary of one of the two instructors in the high school division and supports the music teacher. The auxiliary board is composed of a class of substantial citizens who give a reasonable amount of their time, money, and influence to the school. The people have been taught, by the beautiful example of these men, to stand by the work of the institution; for in which of the three principal churches of the city a nice public collection is taken for, and given to, the auxiliary board every fifth Sunday, and it is not "an after collection." The auxiliary school board raises and expends from seven hundred dollars ($700) to eight hundred dollars ($800) annually. When this board began operation several years ago the colored people had a small three-room building and three poorly paid teachers. They now have a spacious and beautiful, well equipped, two-story, seven-room building and six teachers. A full and thorough seven-year elementary course is given and a good three-year high school curriculum is maintained. Teachers' salaries, though poor, have been increased from time to time, and the entire city seems to be well pleased with the scheme of cooperation and the splendid work done in the school. What has been accomplished in the educational circles in the little city of Tuscumbia can be done with signal success in the great majority of our Southern towns and cities (Trenholm, c. 1911).

African American teachers who taught at both Trenholm and Deshler found that Deshler had a superior physical plant, library, recreational facilities, laboratory facilities, lavatory facilities, courses of instruction, classroom equipment, and cafeteria facilities. This same pattern existed throughout the state of Alabama and many other southern states (Morris & Morris, 2000a).

Mr. Trenholm proposed in his speech that because of the cooperation of the African American community with the public school board in supporting its schools, the White school board might make up the deficits and eventually support the schools for African American children entirely from public funds. There is no evidence that this ever happened. One African American faculty member made the following statement after he began teaching at Deshler: "[We] didn't have to worry about selling peanuts and popcorn to buy anything" (Morris, & Morris, 2000a, p. 162). Yet this was the practice at Trenholm High School from the time it was established until it closed in 1969—separate and unequal from beginning to end.

PART TWO

School Life Before and After Desegregation

CHAPTER FOUR

Leadership Opportunities for African American Children in the School and the Community

PART I PROVIDED the historical context for the Trenholm High School story. Chapter 4 marks the beginning of Part II, which presents a view of what life was like in this segregated African American school community and later in the desegregated school outside the neighborhood.

The Trenholm High School community emphasized very strongly the importance of developing the leadership skills of school-age children as a critical strategy for "uplifting the race." This strategy was carried out using several approaches. First, a picture gallery of famous African Americans adorned the walls of the small auditorium that was the center of activities in the school building. The accomplishments of African Americans such as Frederick Douglass, George Washington Carver, Booker T. Washington, Mary McLeod Bethune, Paul Robeson, Paul Laurence Dunbar, Sojourner Truth, Harriet Tubman, and others were communicated through class content and special programs to inspire students to develop their leadership skills in like fashion to serve and uplift the race. Students were encouraged to believe that with persistence and hard work, they could soar to great heights, just as did these famous African Americans from humble beginnings.

Second, the Trenholm High School community provided a number of activities that would enable students to develop their leadership skills. Students who aspired to speak as did Frederick Douglass or Paul Robeson served as officers in school clubs, were actors in yearly school plays, and delivered speeches in weekly assemblies and local and regional oratorical contests sponsored by community organizations.

Both boys and girls who were inspired by the singing talents of Marian Anderson or Paul Robeson took full advantage of opportunities to develop their musical talents by participating in the school chorus, glee club, talent shows, and choral and band recitals. Students who wanted to be future educators like Mary McLeod Bethune and Booker T. Washington or scientists like George Washington Carver joined such clubs as the Honor Society, the Science Club, New Homemakers of America, the Trade and Industrial Education Club, and the Library Club. While the focus of some of these clubs might not appear to be careers in education, it was very clear that opportunities for African Americans during the segregation period were primarily as teachers in elementary and secondary schools in these areas.

A third approach designed to inspire the development of leadership skills among students was exposing them to programs that featured accomplished national and local African American leaders. Two examples included in this chapter are the visits by George Washington Carver and Mary McLeod Bethune. Students had opportunities to hear their speeches, participate in the programs, and actually see leaders like Dr. Carver engaging in everyday activities. Students were able to see first-hand that these leaders were ordinary individuals who looked like them and who had persisted in making extraordinary contributions not only to the African American community but to the worldwide community. These experiences were designed to enlarge their view of what they could accomplish someday.

Thus, teachers, principals, and parents at Trenholm High School knew the value of extracurricular or co-curricular activities in developing well-rounded children long before recent research findings (Bergstrom & O'Brien, 2001; McLaughlin, 2001; Miller, 2001). Trenholm graduates identified the range of school programs and activities as the number-two factor making their school a good school (Morris & Morris, 2000a). Many of the activities that are considered part of after-school programs today were integrated into the school day at Trenholm while other activities were conducted at the end of the school day. Bergstrom and O'Brien (2001) reported that

> after-school programs have a variety of expected outcomes: to improve students' attitudes toward school, to reinforce basic academic skills, to foster a sense of accomplishment and self-esteem, to improve test scores and grades, to increase engagement in school activities, to improve school attendance, to increase parental involvement, and to create an environment that prevents delinquent behavior and supports students, parents, families, and communities. (p. 33)

Miller (2001) reported that "growing evidence suggests that after-school program participation is associated with higher grades and test scores, especially for low-income children" (p. 7). Miller also found that the most impressive research on the results of after-school programs links participation to significantly lower involvement in risky behaviors, including lower incidence of drinking, smoking, using drugs, having sex, and becoming involved in violence, as well as increased positive behaviors—such as better social and behavioral adjustment, better relations with peers, and more effective conflict resolution strategies—and increased parent involvement. (p. 8)

Newspaper accounts of school-closing and school-opening activities at Trenholm documented the participation of students in co-curricular activities as early as 1887 (*Weekly Dispatch*, 1988) and continued until the school closed in 1969 (Morris & Morris, 2000a). Both boys and girls were involved in a variety of sports activities including football (boys only), basketball, and track and field. Students had opportunities to participate in the marching band, the concert band, and the school chorus. School clubs and organizations included the student council, National Honor Society, National Homemakers of America, Boy and Girl Scouts, the Literary and Drama Club, 4-H Club, Library Club, Trade and Industrial Club, and Y-Teens. Students also developed their speaking skills before audiences during weekly assemblies, spring play performances, and oratorical contests and debates. Whether a part of the school day or after school, these activities were led by teachers from the school with the support and active participation of family and other community members (Morris & Morris, 2000a).

Three graduates of Trenholm High School provide a glimpse of the leadership opportunities for African American children in this school community through participation in these school activities. Lee graduated in 1959, Manual in 1955, and Gloria in 1945.

LEADERSHIP DEVELOPMENT THROUGH
EXTRACURRICULAR ACTIVITIES

One of the highlights of the senior year at Trenholm High School was the spring trip to Washington, D.C. The entire African American community worked together to raise the money to pay for the Greyhound bus and the hotels, food, and entry fees to various historic sites. In 1959, both the senior and junior classes made the trip because the size of the senior class, 19 students, was not enough to fill the bus or to make the trip cost-effective.

Lee, the senior class president, was selected to deliver a short speech at one of the local churches that had agreed to host a fund raiser to support the Washington trip. Since seventh grade, Lee had been president of his homeroom class organization. He was articulate and smart, made good grades, and exhibited leadership skills early in the primary grades both at school and in the community. He always seemed to get the lead male roles in the annual class plays, served as president of the student council, and was captain or co-captain of the football team. Lee also played in the marching and concerts bands, sang in the choir, was a member of the Trade and Industrial Education Club, and a Boy Scout. It was not unusual for students at Trenholm to be involved in multiple extracurricular activities.

Lee selected the title "Why Is Everybody Always Picking on Me?" for his speech to be delivered at the senior fund raiser, scheduled for a Sunday evening at the time when the church's youth group usually met. Lee's speech was based on a popular 1950s song by a group called the Coasters who described a boy named Charlie Brown who seemed to break school and classroom rules rather frequently (Coasters, 1999).

In his presentation, Lee emphasized the need for teenagers to do a realistic self-assessment or to take inventory of their own behaviors before deciding that parents and teachers were merely just "picking on them," especially as they provided guidance in helping them to be productive, happy, and successful adults. Like those of Charlie Brown, the behaviors in which they were sometimes engaged distracted them from the important task of learning and often got them into trouble. Lee, like all other students who gave public speeches, was free to select the topic for his presentation, but always had guidance from a teacher in refining the final product. His fellow classmates were present to cheer him on, along with members of the church. In the spirit of the fifth Sunday rallies that began decades earlier, money was collected after the program to support the seniors' effort to raise the funds needed to pay for their trip to the nation's capital. While this was the only church in the African American community that hosted a program put on by the seniors, several other churches sent donations to support the trip.

Family members and teachers were at the school building to help give the juniors and seniors a big send-off to Washington, DC. Just as the senior classes before them, the students and their chaperones visited the home of George Washington in Mount Vernon, Thomas Jefferson's home at Monticello, Arlington Cemetery, the FBI building, and the Lincoln and Washington Memorials, and toured the White House and took pictures in front of the capitol building. One of the highlights of the trips was dinner and a live show by professional entertainers at a nightclub. The class took pictures there also. Back at home in Alabama, restaurants and hotels were still segregated. In Washington, the students slept at an elegant desegregated hotel and ate meals in very nice restaurants. These high school juniors and seniors really felt like well-respected adults. Of course they still acted like teens from time to time. They had playful pillow fights in the hotel room, sneaked out of their rooms after curfew—and were called back by their watchful chaperones, and smooched on the bus when lights went out for sleeping.

Lee remembered many other opportunities that he and other students at Trenholm High School had to develop public speaking and other leadership skills. Every student from kindergarten through grade 12 had opportunities to speak before an audience during weekly assemblies; annual class plays; band and choral recitals; local, regional, and statewide oratorical contests; academic and athletic banquets; commencement exercises; Boy and Girl Scout activities; and other activities sponsored by the many school clubs in which students were involved.

Oratorical contests at the school and in the region were regular events in which students developed their thinking, writing, and speaking skills. While both boys and girls participated in the contests, the boys with deep, booming voices always seemed to be the top winners. One of those regular winners was Manual, who graduated from Trenholm 4 years earlier than Lee. Manual recalled being eager to get to kindergarten early every day so that he would not be late for the devotional period where they sang and did recitations. He also recalled his participation in an oratorical contest in high school and the encouragement and coaching he received from his teachers. He stated:

> The most profound event in the whole Trenholm High School was when I was doing an oratorical contest in 1954 and I remember Buzz Beasley and Fred Johnson and some other people standing in the back of the auditorium and they said, "Speak loudly and clearly because someday you might want somebody to hear." When I got up there [as part of an American delegation in Hong Kong], I don't know how much I spoke of substance, but I spoke loudly and clearly. And everybody stopped what they were doing and listened . . . . But all I did was what the teachers told me to do. (Morris & Morris, 2000a, p. 63)

Regular speaking and oratorical contests have been important events for developing leadership skills among African American students throughout the country. Dorothy Height, president of the National Council of Negro Women since 1957, tells of an incident that happened when she was a high school student in Pennsylvania competing in a state oratorical contest. As she prepared to attend the contest, her mother told her: "Dorothy, keep yourself together. No matter what happens, just hold yourself together" (in Lanker, 1999, p. 137). She described what happened when they arrived at the hotel in Harrisburg:

When we got to the hotel, they wouldn't let us in. . . . In my speech I talked about Woodrow Wilson and the League of Nations. And I said, "What Brighton said was true. We can't have peace just by having the League of Nations nor any other thing. It's in the hearts of people." Then I said that the message of peace came two thousand years ago. And the messenger could not get into the inn, like I could not get into the hotel that night because I was a Negro. To my surprise, I won the first prize. The irony of this was that they were all white judges. (p. 137).

Students at segregated African American schools in other southern communities had experiences similar to those of the students at Trenholm High School. For example, Ruby Middle Forsythe, a teacher at the Holy Cross Faith Memorial School on Pawleys Island, South Carolina, reported on the activities she provided for her students:

When children start here, regardless of how small they are, they're going to be in the Thanksgiving program, they're going to be in the Easter program, they're going to be in the commencement program. I start them learning a recitation at the age of three. I put them in a little group and give them a piece to learn. Their parents practice with them until they memorize those pieces, and they perform them for the entire school. Some people don't believe that these three-year-olds can get up there and recite four to eight lines, but they do. Facing an audience, giving a recitation, and hearing that applause builds up their confidence and I keep building on that all the time they are with me. (in Foster, 1997, pp. 32–33)

Unlike many students who attended large segregated or desegregated high schools, students at Trenholm could participate in many different activities. They learned to lead activities and to be members of a team whether in club, homeroom, or sports activities. In addition to developing leadership skills, these extracurricular activities contributed to the positive development of students' academic, social, and lifelong leisure skills. Classroom teachers, principals, and other community members worked cooperatively in supporting and providing leadership for student participation in these activities.

Ruby Forsythe had the same goals for her students as those of the teachers, parents, and school community at Trenholm High School. Mrs. Forsythe reminded her students that "they have a responsibility to use their talent to benefit someone other than themselves, and that they have a responsibility to give something back to the community" (in Foster, 1997, p. 35). The La France Club, a student club organized at the Tuscumbia Colored Public School/Trenholm High School in 1907, reinforced these same ideals with their motto, "Lifting as we climb." The La France club was established for young schoolgirls as a source of interest and pleasure for its members and to do some good for humanity. They donated money to the needy, studied the life and works of accomplished African Americans, and performed at special events held at the school building ("A Word," 1908; "Scarf Drill," 1909; "High School Notes," 1908a; 1908b). This tradition of developing leadership skills among the student body continued until the Trenholm building was closed in 1969 and all African American students enrolled at Deshler High School, the desegregated, predominately White school.

At Deshler, African American students had fewer leadership roles than they had had at the segregated African American high school. With only one desegregated high school in Tuscumbia, the number of leadership positions was reduced. And with most positions of leadership determined by popular vote, African American students were very unlikely to hold as many top offices in school clubs and special activities as they had at Trenholm. The segregated African American high school had provided many opportunities for the students to develop leadership skills, an important skill.

GEORGE WASHINGTON CARVER SLEPT HERE

Many communities in the Northeast boast that "George Washington slept here." The African American community in Tuscumbia, Alabama, can boast that "George Washington *Carver* slept here."

Gloria, a 1945 graduate of Trenholm High School, could hardly believe her eyes when she looked out her window to find her mother talking with Dr. George Washington Carver, the famous scientist who had discovered so many uses for the potato and the peanut. She had heard about his work especially during Negro History Week at her school when there were special activities that focused on the accomplishments of famous African American leaders in a variety of professional areas. She recalled Dr. Carver's 1937 visit to Tuscumbia:

> Dr. Carver was at Mrs. Ricks' [Mr. and Mrs. Percy Ricks] next door to us. I never will forget. I must have been 7 or 8 years old. . . . Well, Dr. Carver was up early one morning walking around. And I heard Mama out there talking to him in the front yard. They were talking about flowers and this and that. I never will forget it—tall, thin, with a very high pitched voice. And he later, I think, sent Mama some plants, a yellow cosmos, a yellow flower, planted in the front yard. I never will forget that because he was such a famous man. (Morris & Morris, 2000a, p. 108)

Sheridan (1997) reported that Dr. Carver was invited to speak at the first meeting of the newly organized Wilson Dam Section of the American Chemical Society by George L. Frear, secretary of the organization. Dr. Carver was asked to speak on a topic of interest to both chemists and the general public. The event was held at Sheffield High School (a public high school for Whites located three miles from Tuscumbia) on June 15, 1937, and attracted a large crowd.

Sheridan (1997) also reported on Dr. Carver's arrival in the Muscle Shoals area: "When Dr. Carver and his party arrived in Sheffield in the afternoon of June 14, they were met by Dr. Max Bond, head of TVA's training section and adjuster for colored employers, who made arrangements for their entertainment and accommodations" (p. 1C). Dr. Bond was a neighbor of Mr. and Mrs. Ricks in Tuscumbia where Dr. Carver stayed during his visit. Both Mr. Ricks and Dr. Bond served as members of the Auxiliary School Board for Trenholm High School.

Sheridan made remarks regarding the speech delivered by Dr. Carver on June 15. He stated:

> The audience heard "an interesting and highly instructive lecture" on June 15. Carver concentrated his talk mainly on the many uses he had discovered for the peanut. He displayed several of his products made from peanut oil and orange juice, products resembling milk, cereals, paints varnishes, and wood fillers. He also displayed some paper made from the stems and leaves of the peanut. Carver discussed briefly his experiments with the sweet potato, and displayed a product then on the market—a candy made from the potato. (Sheridan, 1997, p. 1C)

Sheridan (1997) added: "The Wilson Dam Section celebrated its 60th anniversary this year [1997], and continues to sponsor educational programs such as scholarships, high school chemistry contests, awards and technical lectures. But probably none of its other meetings has generated the interest created by Carver's visit" (p. 1C).

Dr. Carver was credited with being the person most responsible for the economic survival of the South. In his laboratory at Tuskegee, he developed many products and processes that expanded the range of agriculture in the southern states (George Washington Carver, 1999a). "In 1914, he used his influence to convince Southern Congressmen to move to other crops besides cotton—a crop being threatened by the boll weevil—and revolutionized southern agriculture"(George Washington Carver, 1999b). Because of his expertise in plant disease and mycology, his advice was sought by countries all over the world. He was offered large salaries to join the companies of Thomas Edison and Henry Ford, but chose instead to remain at Tuskegee to continue his work. He reportedly said: "If I took that money, I might forget my people" (George Washington Carver, 1999b).

Dr. Carver's picture was among the pictures of famous African Americans that adorned the walls of the Trenholm High School auditorium. Because of Abraham Lincoln's efforts to abolish slavery, his picture was also in the collection.

While Dr. Carver was invited to speak in the area by a White group at a White school building, it is very likely that a small section of seating was reserved for African American citizens. At such events where African Americans were allowed to attend, it was the practice at that time to reserve a section of seating in a small anteroom or in a balcony. If the event was sponsored by the African American community, prime seats were reserved for Whites on the platform with the invited guest or in the front seats in the assembly. In any event, African American adults and children beamed with pride when they saw or met someone who looked like them who was an outstanding, respected leader in his chosen field. School-age children were encouraged and stimulated to believe that they too could aspire to such heights.

Dr. Mary McLeod Bethune was another famous African American who visited the Muscle Shoals area ("Thanks," 1981). Dr. Bethune founded a school with $1.50, served as president of Bethune-Cookman College, and was president of the National Council of Negro Women. She was also an adviser to President Franklin Delano Roosevelt and in 1936 was appointed a director in the National Youth Administration by the president (African American, 1999).

On March 17, 1946, Dr. Bethune spoke at the Slater Grammar School (an African American school) in Florence, Alabama, at the invitation of the Tri-Cities (Tuscumbia, Sheffield, and Florence) Branch of the NAACP ("Thanks," 1981). The printed program showed that the Trenholm High School band played at the event, the high school choir sang, and Mrs. Pearl Steward, a teacher at the high school and leader of the NAACP Youth Council, spoke about the work of the local branch. A large number of patrons or sponsors from Tuscumbia were listed on the official program along with those from Sheffield and Florence. The NAACP Youth Council, the Girls Reserve, and the Boy Scouts were ushers for the event.

Gloria also spoke about the People's College, a speaker's bureau established in the African American community, which invited outstanding persons to speak to the community. School-age children attended these events along with their parents and were often participants in the program, as they were at the one where Dr. Bethune spoke. These examples of the cultural activities planned by the African American community were designed to "uplift the race." Students at Trenholm and neighboring segregated African American schools had many opportunities throughout the school year to learn about and to be inspired by the accomplishments of these well-known African Americans, but especially during Negro History Week (now extended to one month, called Black History Month).

Dr. William Hooper Councill, founder and first president, Alabama A&M University. Courtesy of the University Archives, Alabama Agricultural and Mechanical University.

George Washington Trenholm, principal of the Tuscumbia Colored Public School (renamed Trenholm High School in 1921 in his honor), 1896–1916; Supervisor of Negro Education for the State of Alabama, 1916–1920; president of Alabama State University, 1920–1925. Courtesy of Moorland-Spingarn Research Center, Howard University.

Trenholm High School students visiting with Principal Comer E. Leslie at his home. Mr. Leslie was principal from 1927 to 1939. Courtesy of Rubie Leslie Buckingham.

Opening of the new library building built with funds raised under the direction of the Black Auxiliary School Board. Standing is Principal Comer E. Leslie (1927–1939). Sitting from left to right are three members of the auxiliary board: Patsy Graves, George V. Peters, and J. Mack Bonds. Courtesy of George V. Peters.

Trenholm High School Girls Glee Club (c. 1947). Courtesy of
Julia G. Doss.

Trenholm High School faculty at commencement exercises (c. 1949).
FIRST ROW, FROM LEFT: Marie Long, Rubie Leslie Buckingham, Rosa
P. Wesley, Alberta S. Bankston, Ernestyne Whiteside, Magnolia
Watkins, Jessie W. Garrett, and Julia G. Doss. SECOND ROW, FROM
LEFT: John B. Hall, Pattye H. Clark, Sara J. Cleere, Patrick H. Wesley
(principal), Elliot Mabry, Garlor A. Hyler, Adlena Thomas, and
George C. Washington. Courtesy of Fred Johnson.

Trenholm High School 1949 Championship Basketball Team (North
Alabama High School Athletic Association). Standing at back left is
Patrick H. Wesley, principal, and on the right is Coach John Hall.
George Hobson, Athletic Director at Alabama A&M University
and president of the association, is making the award. Courtesy of
Fred Johnson.

Reception for the 1956 graduating class held at the home of Principal
Patrick H. Wesley and Mrs. Rosa P. Wesley. Courtesy of Fred Johnson.

Trenholm High School class of 1957 boarding the bus for their trip to Washington, D.C., during spring break. Family members are there to see them off. Courtesy of Fred Johnson.

Trenholm High School class of 1959 in Washington, D.C. Courtesy of Dorothy B. Johnson.

CHAPTER FIVE

Family and Community Influences in the Lives of School-Age Children

FAMILY AND COMMUNITY involvement was a hallmark at Trenholm High School from its inception in 1877 as the Osborne Academy until it closed in 1969. Parental and community support and involvement were identified by Trenholm graduates as the number-three factor making their school a good school while caring, competent, and committed teachers was noted as number one. And in this instance, family and community included the teachers because the majority of the teachers lived in the community and their children attended the school where they were employed (Morris & Morris, 2000a).

"Parents are their children's first and most influential teachers" is a principle that permeated 20th-century educational literature, especially during the latter half of the century. It is a principle that was taken seriously by parents, family members, and other community residents in the Trenholm school community from the time the school was established until it was closed in 1969.

Chapter 4 provided a broad picture of family and community influence in the Trenholm school community. This chapter provides a closer look at these influences from the viewpoint of Veronica, Erin, Maria, Leann, Ann, Gloria and Manual, all of whom except Maria graduated from Trenholm High School between 1945 and 1959. Maria attended Trenholm during her elementary and junior high years, but completed high school at Deshler in 1969.

A PLACE WHERE YOU FELT LIKE A MEMBER OF A FAMILY

Veronica busily helped her mother prepare dinner for 17 guests who were visitors at their local church that Sunday morning. Since there were no nice local restaurants at which African American visitors could dine or the fast-food restaurants that came later, Veronica's family often welcomed guests to their home for Sunday dinner. While preparing to set the table for dinner, Veronica placed her mom's special cut-glass dinner plates on the large freezer in the kitchen, which was slightly curved at the edges. Because of the vibration created as Veronica and her mother moved swiftly around the kitchen, the dinner plates shifted to the edge and crashed to the floor— no nice dinner plates for the guests. Veronica's mother let out a loud scream, thought for a moment, then marched next door to her neighbor's house to borrow "nice dishes" for the dinner. The day was saved! The neighbor was Veronica's third-grade teacher, Mrs. Rubie Leslie Buckingham, who was also the third-grade teacher for the children who later attended Trenholm High School. Mrs. Buckingham told Veronica's mother that she thought someone had died when she heard the scream next door.

Both Mrs. Buckingham and Veronica's mother planted vegetable and flower gardens every year. As they worked outside in their gardens, they exchanged gardening ideas and kept each other informed about family and community events. Veronica's grandmother and Mrs. Buckingham's mother were best friends for many years, so they did a lot of visiting between the two houses, the kind of visiting that family members do.

The high school coach, Mr. Charles Mahorney, rented a room from the Johnson family, who lived two doors from Veronica's house, next to Mrs. Buckingham. Up through most of the 1960s, single African American teachers (and married teachers who came without their families) who went to Tuscumbia to teach rented rooms from families in the community. There were no vacant houses or apartments available in the area for African Americans to rent or purchase. Veronica's younger brother's classmates and regular playmates after school lived three houses away on the same street with their father, Mr. Patrick Wesley, the principal at the high school, and their mother, Mrs. Rosa Wesley, the sixth-grade teacher.

Veronica's high school biology, chemistry, and physics teacher, Mrs. Deloris McCree, lived across the street with the Eggleston family. Veronica visited with her often just to talk. Teachers like Mrs. McCree always gave good advice about education and other important things about living, just like members of your own family.

Veronica often visited the home of her high school home economics teacher, Mrs. Willie Mae Thompson, when she walked up to the ball field to see African American students or adults play baseball games or practice for interscholastic football games. She would sometimes sit on the front stoop of the newly built brick home to look at the games a few steps away across the street. On one of the days when Veronica was invited inside Mrs. Thompson's house, Veronica recalled seeing for the first time gold flatware and fine white china with a golden ring that matched the flatware and glassware that glistened in the china cabinet. Veronica thought: "One day when I'm a teacher, I'm going to have dishes just like that." Mrs. Thompson was actually Veronica's favorite teacher. She could talk with her in confidence about personal relationships and her plans for the future as you would with a family member. Most of the teachers and their families lived in the community surrounding the school building, as did the majority of the students. Thus, students and their teachers had many opportunities to interact on a daily basis beyond the classroom walls.

Erin saw his teachers as part of a family who wanted their students to achieve and succeed, just as his own family did. He stated: "I think we had teachers there who had our interest at heart. They wanted us not only to do well, but to move further along than they did themselves" (Morris & Morris, 2000a, p. 50)—just like good parents. He also spoke of graduates' encounters with their former teachers when they went back home for visits while attending college. He remarked: "I can remember going off to college and coming home. They were proud to see us. They wanted to hear all the things we had learned in school and where we had been" (Morris & Morris, 2000a, p. 51). When Manual spoke of his favorite teacher, Mr. Willie Lee Green, he stated: "I think he felt like the success or non-success of a student was a reflection on him as a teacher" (Morris & Morris, 2000a, p. 57)—just as parents feel that the success or nonsuccess of their child is a reflection on them.

Maria communicated the family atmosphere she experienced while a student at Trenholm:

> At Trenholm, I think there was a sense of that somehow everybody was a part of a family, everybody knew everybody else, and you know, cared about what happened to people. The students cared about each other, felt like you belonged. The teachers cared about you. . . . Trenholm was a family. You knew it when you were there. And it was not just during the school day, but all the time. You felt like people cared about you. . . . Everybody just looked out for each other all the time. (Morris & Morris, 2000a, p. 57)

Maria also talked about the long-term effect that the family atmosphere at Trenholm had on those who were part of the school community. She stated:

> School is the link that runs through us all. And it keeps us forever connected. You can be anywhere in the country. And if you run into somebody that went to Trenholm High School, I believe I have got open arms and an open door. So I think that school is sort of like blood, family.

In their interview and questionnaire responses, Trenholm graduates indicated that their teachers showed that they cared about their students in a variety of ways. Their favorite teachers maintained orderly classrooms, were fair, were competent in their subject areas, made practical applications of subject matter, had high expectations of students, and made learning fun. Teachers also served as advisors for clubs, coaches for athletic events, and sponsors of social activities that were planned by the school. This same ethic of caring was extended beyond the classroom as teachers, principals, and family members worked cooperatively to establish school related and community organizations that often provided civic, social, recreational, and leadership activities for the adults as well as met a variety of needs of school-age children (Morris & Morris, 2000a).

Like Lorraine Lawrence, teachers at Trenholm High School knew that being good teachers of African American children entailed more than imparting subject matter. Lawrence stated:

> Teachers are responsible for imparting subject matter, and they really need to know a subject inside out if they're going to teach it well. But if teachers are going to be effective with students, they have to be concerned with more than simply teaching their subject matter. They have to help students see their potential, see beyond their current situation to the possibilities that are out in the world, which, because of their inexperience, students may be unable to see. In order to do that teachers have to be concerned with their students' feelings and emotions. (in Foster, 1997, p. 96)

What Lawrence talked about and what teachers did at Trenholm High School is also what good parents do for their own children, what families do for their own.

A COMMUNITY OF EDUCATORS:
TEACHERS, FAMILY MEMBERS, AND OTHERS

Who were the "real" educators? Many parents and community residents had not received the kind of education their children got at Trenholm High School—the school they actively supported throughout its existence. However, they were educators, as were Winson and Dovie Hudson, two activist sisters from rural Carthage, Mississippi, who worked on behalf of children. Winson Hudson stated:

> I've never walked down the hall with a cap and gown on, but I walked down a hall in Washington and I lobbied for student loans, and I lob-

bied for Social Security, and I lobbied for teachers' pay raises, and I've helped you get equal pay right here in the county, so I'm the educator." (in Lanker, 1999, p. 165)

Leann's parents were "real" educators. They purchased a set of encyclopedias for their home at a time when there were few up-to-date books in their school library and the public library downtown was reserved for Whites only. Leann and her brothers must have read those books from cover to cover. The pictures were in color and for certain entries there were transparency overlays that showed the stages of certain processes, like the growth of the human baby prior to birth. There was nothing like this in the high school library.

Leann's father also read the encyclopedias from cover to cover. He would spend hours lying in bed reading books, newspapers, and union contracts. He had a habit of keeping newspaper clippings of little-known facts in his billfold and taking them out to use in conversation with his children and others. He might begin with: "Did you know that . . . ?" Friends and neighbors always seemed to enjoy his company. He was up-to-date on world affairs, was humorous; he made you laugh and cry as he engaged you in conversation. Leann and her brothers saw their dad read those little union contract agreements (pocket-size booklets) in preparation for negotiations and observed him as he practiced his presentations in front of the big mirror over the fireplace in the living room.

Leann's mother read her Bible and Sunday school materials to prepare for teaching young children at church and to give lectures and make presentations for ladies' Bible classes. She wrote her speeches in longhand and did lots of oral practice prior to the day of the event. Neither of Leann's parents was a high school graduate, and they didn't always use correct grammar, but they were active educators in their home and in their community. They were regular participants in the PTA and band-booster activities at the high school and the community voters' league. They encouraged and supported each of their children to earn a college education— and they did. Leann and her brothers are practicing professionals holding several graduate degrees among them. They all are avid readers, deliver public speeches on a regular basis as part of their work and as contributions to the communities in which they live, and are teachers in their church. And they enjoy great conversation, especially the kind that seems to include both laughing and crying. There is no doubt that their parents were real educators.

Ann really enjoyed reading, but like most of the students at Trenholm, she found few books at home. However, there were some African American neighbors who had well-stocked libraries in their homes who made their books available to children in the community. Ann spoke of one of her neighbors, Mr. John L. Griffin, who subscribed to *National Geographic* for her. She stated:

> He was very interested in the school and kids learning to speak correctly and write correctly. . . . He often wanted to make sure that I read it. And he would show me pictures and one picture in particular had four cocker spaniels on it. And he cut the picture out and said I want you to write a paper on what you see when you look at this picture. And I wrote the paper and he corrected it. Grammar and whatever and I took it to school and showed it to my teacher and I had pasted the picture of the cocker spaniel on the front of my paper like a booklet and she was thrilled with it. She said it was such a good paper, she gave me an "A" on it. (Morris & Morris, 2000a, p. 113)

Ann also recalled her visits to the high school building for Whites (Deshler High School) where her dad was janitor. While her dad did his work, she read many books and explored the resources that were sorely missing from the school library at the segregated African American high school that she attended. And when she had term papers to do, her dad borrowed books from the Deshler library (unofficially of course), so that she had adequate resources to develop very good papers. Ann's dad was also a member of the Auxiliary School Board at Trenholm High School.

Frank and Alice Graves were parents and community activists in the Trenholm High School community. They served on the "Black Board" (as it was often called) for Trenholm High School, boarded teachers in their home, and held receptions for graduating seniors in their home, as well. Gloria, their youngest daughter, reported that her mother was an avid reader and often shared her resources with children, teachers, and other adult members of the community, both White and African American (Morris & Morris, 2000a). Gloria noted that

> Mama took every magazine that ever came out on the market. . . . Some of the teachers would come to Mama to get specific periodicals that they did not even have in the library. They used her resources all the time. Because she always had the house lined with books and magazines. She was in a monthly book club when it first came into being. (Morris & Morris, 2000a, p. 114)

Manual's dad and his two chemist colleagues provided chemicals and lent equipment to the science teacher at the high school to enable the teacher to carry out hands-on chemistry experiments for the students. Money for supplies and equipment was not made available through the school or school district budgets. Both Erin and Manual recalled the informal club activities that Mrs. Betty Thompson held in her home each Saturday for school-age boys in the Trenholm community. She read Bible scriptures and other stories to the boys, and served some refreshments. About 15 young boys from the community met weekly at her home (Morris & Morris, 2000a).

It is evident that African Americans in the Trenholm school community saw themselves as a community of learners and educators, side-by-side with school administrators and teachers. Parents, family members, and other community residents were "real educators," as were the principals and teachers hired by the school district. Students saw themselves as members of a family both in the school building and in the community where everyone cared for and was concerned for one another. This family atmosphere was lost when African Americans students began attending the desegregated high school in their town.

CHAPTER SIX

The Unmet Promises of School Desegregation

THE STORIES ABOUT the unmet promises of school desegregation in this small southern town come primarily from the memories of Vanessa, Ann, Erin, and Wilson. These former students completed grades 1–12 at Trenholm High School and graduated between 1957 and 1960. At different periods from 1964 through the 1990s, children of these graduates also attended Trenholm, as well as the desegregated elementary, middle, and high schools in Tuscumbia. Additional data that support or enhance their stories are summarized from interviews, questionnaires, and other documents used for this research project.

INEQUALITY BEFORE DESEGREGATION

For most of the 20th century, African Americans and Whites growing up in Tuscumbia and other communities throughout this country were taught through words and deeds—literally through life experiences—that everything White and for Whites was better or superior. Vanessa remembered only too well some of these experiences of growing from a young child into early adulthood in this small southern community.

> We [African Americans] knew that they [Whites] had well built, comfortable, and spacious homes because we cleaned them, and cared for their young and old in them. We mowed their well-manicured lawns, trimmed their shrubbery, and weeded their flower and vegetable gardens. We knew they had elegant, well-appointed restaurants because we scrubbed the floors, we washed the dishes, we cooked the food to be served by White waitresses in the lovely dining areas and we ate our food in the kitchen once all the needs of the White customers were met. We knew they had access to the finest hotels because we washed the sheets, made the

beds, cleaned the toilets, and vacuumed the lush carpets. We knew about the services that were available at the drugstores in our town where we purchased our prescriptions and other sundries, but were unwelcome in the soda shop area where Whites sat and enjoyed a soothing milk shake or a hot cup of coffee or hot chocolate on a cold winter day.

We went to the same doctor offices and clinics, where we sat in hard uncomfortable chairs in small, dingy waiting rooms the size of closets, while White patients waited for the same doctors where they enjoyed the comfort of luxurious leather chairs and sofas in spacious rooms with the opportunity to read current popular magazines. We established checking and saving accounts at the local banks where we cleaned the buildings, but were denied jobs as bank tellers and loan officers.

Whites enjoyed the recreational facilities of the Big Spring Park with a variety of play equipment for the children and park benches for playing games and eating. We always knew about the big barbecues that they held because one of our African American neighbors did the cooking. And our small, ill equipped "park" was just a few steps across the highway, so we could see the festivities with our own eyes. In the early days, there was also a swimming pool at Spring Park that was enjoyed by the White citizens and their children. Young African Americans in the community who learned to swim developed their skills in dangerous, unsupervised creeks, ponds, and lakes.

Vanessa remembered seeing her mom and dad cry following the swimming deaths of her 11-year-old brother and 16-year-old cousin in one of the local unsupervised swimming holes. She was 6, a first grader, at the time of these tragic deaths. At the end of the seventh grade, one of Vanessa's classmates and her classmate's mother drowned in one of the local lakes. These are memories that continue to be part of her dreams nearly 50 years later.

In the fall of 1948, Vanessa enrolled in first grade at Trenholm. What was it like attending this segregated African American school located three blocks from her home? Vanessa agreed with the majority of the graduates about the number one factor that made Trenholm a good school: It was the caring, competent, and dedicated teachers. Vanessa already knew almost all of the teachers when she enrolled in first grade. They were her neighbors. She went to church with them and she saw them at the grocery stores and at social and recreational events in her community. She played in their homes with their children and their children played baseball and football in her spacious yard. She saw the teachers at assembly programs and at school plays when she attended the private community kindergarten that met on the campus of Trenholm High School.

Like other graduates, Vanessa believed that the teachers at Trenholm cared about who their students were, where they came from, and where they were going. Graduates reported that their teachers had high expectations for the students, were competent teachers, and made learning fun. This ethic of caring evidenced by teachers was not only present in the classroom, but exhibited as they sponsored extracurricular activities at the school building and community activities through social and civic clubs designed to benefit schoolchildren and adults, with the common goal of "uplifting the race." Students were encouraged to do well in school (especially academically) as they were admonished by their teachers that "they had to be twice as good as Whites" to get the same jobs. Trenholm graduates discovered that they were well prepared academically as they pursued bachelor's and advanced degrees at historically Black colleges and predominately White colleges and universities, throughout this nation (Morris & Morris, 2000a).

The 1955 accreditation report by the Southern Association of Colleges and Schools attested to the powerful relationships that existed in this school community: "Certain limitations in physical facilities are handicapping, but evidences in pupil-teacher relationships, pupil pride, pupil respect and attitude reflect a very wholesome atmosphere" (*Report*, 1955, p. 36). The committee commended the school "staff and student body on the fine school spirit, attitude, and rapport between pupil-pupil, pupil-teacher, and pupil-teacher-administrator (p. 39).

Trenholm High School could not have operated effectively without the active involvement and support of families and the community. Families and community residents raised money to purchase land, build buildings, pay teachers' salaries, and purchase equipment and instructional resources. From the time the school was established in the 1877 until it closed in 1969, it never had the physical plant or instructional resources equal to the White school buildings in the community, even with the added financial support of the African American community.

As a school-age child, Vanessa had never been inside the three White school buildings in Tuscumbia and neither had most African American children or many of the teachers who taught at Trenholm High School. However, African Americans who cleaned the buildings and cooked lunch for the students and teachers in the segregated White buildings had a glimpse of the materials and equipment that were available for instruction in those buildings. And the resources were in abundance in comparison with what they saw at their children's school in their community.

Ann was one of the few African American students (before 1965) to have a first-hand glimpse of the physical facilities in the White school buildings, as she read in "their" library while her father cleaned the building. Ann noted two things that were different in the White high school building:

They had markers [magic markers]. I had never seen markers in school. We had chalk. The bathrooms had doors on the front. They had real closed stalls and our stalls [at Trenholm] were open. They had a long line of face bowls where several girls could go in and wash their hands. . . . And that part was separated from where you had to go to the stall. That was totally different from our bathrooms. . . . And no kind of security [stalls with doors that you could be locked while in use]. You couldn't go in and lock the door so no one could come in on you.

Ann also remembered not having a standard-sized gym for most of the years Trenholm High was operational (a new gym was built in 1960 and torn down in 1969 when the school building was closed).

We had one big room in the middle of our school and all the classrooms were around it. And that one big room was our multipurpose center. It was our gym, it was our ballroom, it was our chapel, and it was our place for graduation. It was the place of big funerals, basketball games, everything, in that one room.

Erin had an occasion to visit Deshler (the White high school) when he and some other students from Trenholm went down to pick up some used football equipment and uniforms. Erin stated:

I recognized that there were some inadequacies in the education because I had the occasion to go to the White school in the summer while I was there [a student at Trenholm]. I saw some of the laboratories that they had; the biology and chemistry laboratories that they had and we had nothing even close to the facilities that they had. And I liked science; that was always of interest to me. And even the classroom facilities, the library, the gym, all those things were far superior and I had a chance to observe those and I knew that there was something going on when I looked at ours. . . . We used old hand me down football uniforms and hand me down books that they no longer wanted. (Morris & Morris, 2000a, p. 70)

Erin further commented:

Every year we would get one or two new books that were not hand me down books from the White schools. So I knew that there was something amiss in terms of what we should have had. But of course it was difficult to put it all together.

Wilson believed that his education at Trenholm was shortchanged primarily because Whites controlled the monetary resources for the schools. His three children completed their education at the desegregated schools in the community. He remarked: "I figured as an all Black school, we were being short changed on education. . . . I just wished I could have attended Deshler, integrated. I really wish that. Opportunity was so much greater, everything was greater. Being an all white school [Deshler], the opportunity was there for them" [his children]. (Morris & Morris, 2002).

Vanessa, like many students attending Trenholm, did not get a glimpse of what went on inside the White school buildings in Tuscumbia, but she saw that the buildings were larger, with well-kept grounds and lots of playground equipment in good repair. The White school had a standard-size gym and a football stadium next to the school building where they practiced and played football and held track meets, and which could be used for other activities during the school day. Trenholm scheduled their football games and track meets after Deshler's schedule was set, but practiced on their dusty and eroded school playground or after school at the "ball field," a poorly developed recreational area set aside for African American citizens located three blocks east of the school building.

Thus, with all the past lived experiences, it seemed logical for many African Americans to believe that with legal desegregation of schools their children would finally get an education that was equal to that of Whites in their community. School desegregation ushered in by the *Brown* decision was viewed by many as the saving grace to deliver African American children from the perilous wilderness conditions of segregated schools to the promised land of integrated schooling. Lisa Delpit agrees that "the real reason for the school desegregation struggle was to gain the economic benefits and resources for black children that were commonly provided for white children" (in Foster, 1997, p. ix).

AFTER DESEGREGATION

So what did African American students find when they began attending the desegregated, predominately White high school across town? When

African American children began attending desegregated schools in Tuscumbia in 1965, they and their parents found the physical plant, technological equipment, and other instructional resources to be superior to that at the segregated African American school—separate and unequal. These resources were visible evidence of the community's support for a quality education. While physical resources are important indicators, they are not absolute proof that a quality education exists within the walls of a school building. There are other factors, in addition to the tangible things, that may not be readily visible but are absolutely critical in determining the quality of education for children in K-12 schools.

We reported (Morris and Morris, 2000a) that while African American students in Tuscumbia were able to survive and graduate from Deshler during the early years of desegregation (1965 to 1980), many never felt they fit in or felt as safe and secure as they had at Trenholm. It was not "their school" as Trenholm was. They felt as if they were in an alien environment. The sense of belonging that they experienced at Trenholm did not exist at Deshler. They did not find the family atmosphere that was quite evident to them at Trenholm. White teachers, administrators, and children treated African American parents and their children with hostility. African American students felt that some teachers were insensitive in the manner in which they handled classroom topics related to the history and experiences of African Americans.

Parents could no longer exercise their strong leadership in support of school activities through the PTA as they had at Trenholm. A previous principal had disbanded the PTA at Deshler High School because of conflicts among the membership. And because of the "new rules" for participating in school clubs and other extracurricular activities, African American students became primarily followers, rather than leaders, while some chose not to participate at all (Morris & Morris, 2000a).

The social and emotional losses of desegregation have not often been weighed as critical factors in the ultimate goal of academic achievement. Peebles (2000) stated that "vast numbers of people—adults and children—were emotionally affected by desegregation. It made a profound impression upon individual lives and families, on all of us " (p. 89). When asked to describe how they felt when they learned that the Trenholm High School buildings were torn down, Trenholm graduates indicated that they felt angry, bad, cheated, defeated, depressed, devastated, disregarded, hurt, remorseful, robbed, speechless, surprised, confused, shocked, and unhappy (Morris, 1993).

In a later work we reported further (Morris & Morris, 2000a) on the emotional responses of the African American community when the Trenholm buildings were closed and demolished:

When Trenholm was closed and the buildings were demolished, the grief and feelings of sadness were not so much for the "bricks and mortar" but for what they stood for, the blood, sweat, and tears of hundreds of African Americans—teachers, principals, parents, and other community residents—who worked, struggled, and sacrificed to make Trenholm a good school for their children despite the allocation of "separate and unequal" resources by the school board. And in this country, America, we build monuments to commemorate the achievements and struggles of people for good; we don't tear them down. (p. 170)

Walker (1998) agreed that there should be a merger of cultures in the desegregation of schools. However, in many communities throughout the country, African Americans are forced to adopt the rules and regulations of the formerly all-White school. This is precisely what happened at Deshler. Trenholm graduates reported a great sense of loss of symbols around which the community had rallied for so many decades.

When Trenholm was closed and African American students enrolled at Deshler, they lost their school colors, their symbols, and their mascot. All of these symbols were important socially and emotionally to the students and to the African American community. It was around these symbols that the school community rallied. There was no longer the maroon and gold and the Trenholm Wildcats, but red and white and the Deshler Tigers. One teacher remarked: "We went from maroon and gold, and the name change. Deshler was not supposed to remain Deshler. Since we lost Trenholm, we were supposed to go with some other name, but didn't." He indicated that this issue had been decided in the joint school and community meetings that had taken place in preparation for desegregation, but it did not happen. Another teacher remarked: "We were not completely integrated." Again, the African American community was on the losing end. (Morris & Morris, 2000a, p. 168)

The lack of positive teacher-student and student-student relationships, limited involvement in extracurricular activities, and decreased involvement of African American families and community in the life of the school were some of the "invisible" factors that affected the ability of both African American and White students to focus on educational tasks—and hence affected the quality of education each student received in the desegregated setting. Students were inhibited from reaching their potential in this environment. This certainly is not what African American parents and children expected when schools were desegregated.

CHAPTER SEVEN

A Virus in the Folklore: Skin Color and Student Preference

THIS CHAPTER INCLUDES stories from both the segregated African American school community and the desegregated high school that African American students began attending in 1965 when the school district adopted a Freedom of Choice plan. Valerie and Marie tell how skin color and student preference affected relationships both inside the classroom and in the African American community. Marie relates additional stories about her experiences in the desegregated school setting. Valerie completed grades 1–12 at Trenholm High School and graduated in 1959. Maria spent her elementary and junior high school years at Trenholm and graduated from Deshler High School in 1969.

THE DISCRIMINATION VIRUS

The cold virus has been around for centuries. Scientists have not found a cure for it, and it keeps passing from person to person, year after year. Medical science knows only how to treat the symptoms. Just as the cold virus affects the body and the spirit, the "discrimination virus" poisons the mind and the spirit. Like the cold virus, the discrimination virus cannot be seen with the naked eye, yet it is highly infectious and can pass from one person to another very rapidly, often without recipients being aware that they have been infected. However, the discrimination virus, based on skin color, differs from the cold virus in one very important way: The cold virus may be active in an individual's body for only one or two weeks per year, and maybe not even every year. But the discrimination virus has the potential for affecting the life of a victim everyday for a lifetime. You can't see the virus but victims can recognize how it sounds, how it feels, and they experience the results of the infection in their lives.

DISCRIMINATION IN THE AFRICAN AMERICAN COMMUNITY

Valerie remembers how this virus was communicated in a little poem while she was growing up in Tuscumbia during the 1940s and 1950s.

> *If you're white, you're right,*
> *If you're yellow, you're mellow,*
> *If you're brown, stick around,*
> *If you're black, get back.*

Valerie did detect some signs in her school life and other places that indicated some favoritism based on skin tones among African Americans. These clues seemed to get stronger as she got older. For example, a student named Beverly who had not been a member of her Community Kindergarten class with Miss Doss enrolled in Valerie's first-grade class. Beverly was considered a high yellow by those affected with the virus, and had long braids. It seemed that all the girls were competing to make Beverly their very best friend. There was even a minor fracas on the playground during recess among the first-grade girls related to this new friendship.

In second grade, Pamela enrolled in Valerie's class. She was from another state and she looked just like the daughters of the white grocery store owners in the African American community. She looked white, had long braids of straight hair that ended about the middle of her back, and she didn't have her hair straightened with a hot comb like the rest of the girls in her class. She could wash, dry, and braid. She reminded Valerie of Heidi, a character in one of the storybooks they had read in class. In the upper elementary grades both Beverly and Pamela were junior majorettes with the high school marching band. There were a few brown or slightly dark girls from Valerie's class who were majorettes also, but they seemed to be able to do special things like turn somersaults very well or make very high steps as the band marched down the street. It seemed to Valerie that an unusual number of the junior and senior majorettes were yellow or very fair, and often had long straight hair (after long bouts with the hot comb) or natural curls (then called "good hair").

As Valerie grew into her teen years, she noticed that the girls with fair skin seemed to have many more of the boys vying for their affections. And when one of the boys was able to have a girl who looked like Beverly or Pamela as a steady girlfriend, he appeared to have achieved special status among the other teenage boys in school. For many years, the homecoming queens at the high school appeared to be mostly fair-skinned girls and as Valerie began reading *Jet Magazine* and *Ebony*, she also noticed that the majority of the homecoming queens at Black colleges were very fair.

Valerie recalled that Mr. Miller, who taught a family living class during their junior and senior years in high school, chided them as they discussed marriage. He said that students needed to consider the color of the person they planned to marry—in the best interest of the children that would be born in their families. Without his saying the words directly, students understood that he was talking about skin complexion. Dark-skinned children did not appear to have the same value as light-skinned children in our community and in our school. And when Valerie looked around her community, many of the African American men who were considered to be well off (doctors, undertakers, professionals at TVA) had very fair-skinned wives, even though many of the men were brown-skinned or very dark. Fair-skinned girls and women seemed to have a higher value in the African American community than those who were brown or very dark. Valerie recalled hearing one of her brother's friends say that "the only thing a black girl could tell me is where to find a yellow one." Too often she had heard people say: "You know Jennifer is dark, *but* she's pretty." She never heard anyone say: "You know Pamela is fair, *but* she's pretty." It was implied that a fair-skinned girl *was* pretty while a dark-skinned girl *was not.*

Valerie also heard adults in her community recall on several occasions incidents related particularly to the skin complexion of women. The story was told of one proud mother who spread the word in the community that she wanted everyone to come to see her new daughter-in-law from Mississippi. She reportedly remarked with pride: "She looks just like a White woman." On the other hand, another young man brought his dark-skinned bride home to meet his family. The story was told that his fair-skinned mother fainted at the sight of her new daughter-in-law. The virus was rampant in Valerie's community.

Maria lived in Valerie's neighborhood and completed the elementary and junior high grades at Trenholm High School. She completed grades 9 through 12 at Deshler, the desegregated high school. She recalled how skin complexion played a role in preferential treatment at the segregated African American school:

> There tended to be a preference to lighter skinned kids. And the girls particularly. Lighter skin with long hair gave you an advantage with the teachers. Or it certainly was perceived that way. . . . It was little things . . . the things that showed whatever particular teachers had students to do that showed this is the person upon whom they are bestowing their favor at any given time. . . . You get to do the erasers [clean chalk board erasers], or you get to call everybody to order, you get to maybe call roll. . . . You don't know what really happened relative to grades, to tell the truth. . . . And

teachers would call on them. . . . If two kids had their hands up, they [teachers] would call on that one [the lighter-skinned student]. . . . I felt like it was certainly not fair and it made you feel like you had to work a little harder . . . there was some inferiority there because you were not as light skinned. . . . But dark skinned kids, little girls with dark skin and short hair, had really a tougher time. And that was pretty obvious to me. (Morris & Morris, 2000a, p. 60)

The virus of preferential treatment of fair-complexioned African Americans has invaded the lives of many villages and communities throughout this country, from border to border—East to West and North to South. In her book *Black Teachers on Teaching* (1997), Michele Foster deals with this same issue:

Not all black teachers are sympathetic to their young scholars. Color distinctions between light-skinned black teachers and their dark-complexioned pupils were sometimes enacted in the classroom with teachers favoring lighter pupils over the darker ones. (p. xlvi)

Foster quoted remarks made by one of the teachers she interviewed regarding attitudes about color in African American communities:

The teachers at Lincoln High School were black but for the most part they were light-skinned. There was a lot of color consciousness in my community and in my school. I'm the brown-skinned child, one of the darkest children in my family. Even as a child, I was serious. The neighbors used to comment, "That little dark one—she's too serious; we need to watch her—she doesn't laugh when the rest of them laugh." In those days people equated being dark skinned with being evil. I always resented that. (p. xlvii)

Several dark-skinned African American women who have been important change agents in this country spoke about this issue in Brian Lanker's *I Dream a World* (1999). The poet Gwendolyn Brooks stated: "My poem, 'Ballard of Pearl May Lee,' examines the whole thing from the viewpoint of the dark-complexioned black woman. It expresses the way a lot of women of my complexion feel. They have been neglected in favor of light-complexioned black women" (p. 47).

Valerie recalled that in her community during the 1940s and 1950s *black* was a fighting word. And the ultimate insult was to be called an "old black dog." If you were the person dispensing the venom, you knew you had to be ready to fight or run. However, many parents armed their children with antivirus defenses. Some of Valerie's dark-skinned classmates would remark when called *black* as an insult: "The blacker the berry, the sweeter the juice." This phrase of pride seemed to be used more by boys than girls. In her book *Lanterns* (1999), Marian Wright Edelman noted that she first heard this phrase used by Dr. Mary McLeod Bethune, a college president, adviser to President Franklin Roosevelt, and one of her mentors. Edelman stated: "She [Dr. Bethune] exuded great pride in her God-painted very Black skin" (p. 125). Edelman also recalled how Mayor Unita Blackwell's (Mayersville, Mississippi) mother had armed her to deal with this virus of preferential treatment based on skin color. Mayor Blackwell remarked:

> When I was young I had a Black boyfriend but he was very light-skinned and I was very dark. He had a hard time with other children because he liked someone so dark and others were jealous because I had a light-skinned boy friend. . . . I went on to understand this vicious race problem in this country and how color was so important even in our own race. (p. 97)

DISCRIMINATION AT THE DESEGREGATED HIGH SCHOOL

Maria recalled how this virus raised its vicious head when she enrolled in the desegregated high school (Deshler) in Tuscumbia. She stated how some White students showed their displeasure at African Americans' attending "their" school. She said: "You walked in and you sat down and people next to you got up." Maria also talked about what happened when students were provided instruction in giving CPR in their physical education class.

> We didn't have anything to put over the dummy's mouth, you just sort of did that behind people, and you wiped off the dummy's mouth. And I refused to do it. And they [*White students*] found that surprising. I can remember one of the kids saying, "Well it would be different if I did not want to do that behind YOU. But for you not to want to do that behind me, being a nigger and all." (Morris & Morris, 2000a, p. 125)

White teachers in the desegregated school were also active in spreading the virus. Maria noted one such incident that took place in a social studies class studying Jefferson Davis and the Confederacy.

> She [the teacher] was saying that he [Jefferson Davis] felt in order to bring the Confederacy back to where it needed to be and to resolve all of these problems, he wanted to put the "nigra" and she would

always say that, a lot of them said "nigra," most of them would not say Negro at the time. She said that he wanted to put them on the boat and send them all back to Africa . . . but the slaves did not want to go back, they liked it here. She said, "Maria, you would not want to go back to Africa, would you?" And I said, "I beg your pardon, but I have never been to Africa." And I said, "I guess I'm not any more interested in going back to Africa than you are to going back to England or Scotland or wherever you came from." And I got sent to the principal's office. (Morris & Morris, 2000a, p. 125)

Maria continued by describing the consequences of this incident:

I think first of all, it was shocking to her. She was very upset by my having said that. And she said that she did not mean that to be insulting, and I told her that I took it that way. But I will be honest. I think that was a point in time that many of the students had a different regard for me after that point. I mean, it was pretty obvious that I did not intend to take a lot of stuff. And I guess one thing, at age 14 to say anything like that to a teacher, you know. They were looking at me like ooooh!! (Morris & Morris, 2000a, p. 125)

She indicated that when she went to the office, the principal "understood why I would feel that way about it. He did not think it was an appropriate thing for her to have asked me." Thus, no action was taken against Maria (Morris & Morris, 2000a).

Maria also recounts entering one of her classrooms following the assassination of Dr. Martin Luther King, Jr. Someone had written on the chalkboard, "The king is dead, long live the king." In the class discussion that followed, she indicated that her teacher was offended by the use of the word "assassinated" when referring to Dr. King. She noted that the teacher said:

He did not rise to the level to be assassinated. He did not rise to the level of importance. And that was another point in time where we had that discussion. And she said that assassination was a word that was reserved for use when you are talking about heads of state. And I disagreed with her. I told her that was not true, that it was a word that was used when somebody took it upon themselves to kill somebody whose existence rose to the level of being a leader, whether it was an elected leader or not, but being a leader and somebody who made an impact on society, and that he certainly did this. But she did insist that, to the extent that it was talked about in her class, nevertheless it was her room, and the word "assassinated" would not be used. And I remember saying, "Well, you are right, you are the teacher and it is your classroom." . . . You could not feel like you needed to feel. And I just remember just feeling stifled because there was no discussion of it, other than that one teacher who then was making sure that we understood that his [Dr. King's] place was not one of importance. (Morris & Morris, 2000a, p. 126)

In the last decades of the 20th century, school districts, colleges and universities, and other public and private agencies developed programs to attack the virus of preferential treatment based on race. They used sensitivity training, diversity workshops, and cultural immersion programs. However, as we begin a new century, the virus is alive and well and too often, it is as vicious as it was at the beginning of the 20th century. This insidious virus of preferential treatment of students based on race or skin complexion has the potential to stunt the intellectual, emotional, and social development of its victims. Those who discriminate are also victims because in the process of spreading the virus, they develop a false sense of superiority and deprive themselves of important relationships that could be mutually beneficial.

The net result of this poisonous infection is a loss of human resources and talents to individuals, families, communities, and the country. America can no longer afford these losses. Wolk (2000) asserts that "despite nearly half a century of bitter litigation in many states, the fact remains that the quality of education that children receive depends largely on where they live, *the color of their skin,* and the affluence of their family" (p. 15; emphasis added).

While there appeared to be some rather subtle practices of student preferences based on skin color in the segregated African American high school, race became "the issue" in the desegregated school setting. African American students did not feel that their White teachers cared about them or were committed to meeting their needs as students. The positive teacher-student and student-student relationships that had existed at Trenholm were not present at Deshler High School. African American students felt as if they were in an alien environment, a quantum leap backward from the family atmosphere they had experienced at Trenholm.

CHAPTER EIGHT

The Myth of the Unusual Negro

WHEN TRENHOLM STUDENTS began attending Deshler, the desegregated high school, and the predominately White college in a neighboring town, they came face-to-face with the concept of the "unusual Negro" of the 1960s and 1970s. Maria, Fred Johnson, Wendell, Valerie, and Rubie Leslie Buckingham related their stories about this concept. Maria attended both Trenholm and Deshler, while Wendell and Valerie attended Trenholm. Mr. Johnson and Mrs. Buckingham taught at Trenholm, as well as in desegregated schools in Tuscumbia.

It appears that some Whites believed that the phrase "unusual Negro" was a compliment; many African Americans perceive the phrase as a put-down. The idea may communicate: "You're special, not like the other people who look like you and talk like you. You're more like us [Whites]. So it's okay for you to work with us or go to school with us or to live next door to us. After all, one or two is okay. There is no real threat."

SOME "UNUSUAL" NEGROES

Several students who attended Trenholm High School, the segregated African American high school in Tuscumbia, experienced the "unusual Negro" myth in the desegregated school setting. For example, Maria indicated that for the first 3 years of desegregation at Deshler High School, she was the only African American in each of her classes. She stated:

> They [Whites] accepted that I was what they called smart, but viewed it as something that was a novelty. . . . Particularly after the first six weeks in class, they thought that I was at least not what they thought that we [African Americans] were supposed to be. (Morris & Morris, 2000a, p. 126)

Maria's statements infer that White students did not expect African Americans to be smart. If they were, they were "unusual." Conversely then, it could be inferred that Whites expected "usual"—ordinary or regular African Americans—to be dumb or have poor academic skills. Marie also noted her experience with a science teacher at the desegregated high school who left her in charge when he left the room. He recognized that she was far ahead of the other students (all White) in her class, and she noted that this was a very unusual situation (Morris & Morris, 2000a).

Fred Johnson, the last principal at Trenholm High School, recalled an unusual Negro incident that happened shortly after all African American students were assigned to Deshler. He stated:

> A few Black children got aroused about something. . . . They were going to call a meeting with Mr. Donley, the principal, and they used Flora . . . as spokesperson. And he asked me to come in. . . . And . . . when he got through that meeting, he said, "Man, I never had a child talk to me like this." And it just really knocked him off his feet! That girl, she sat there and I mean she had it down pat. She said, "Mr. Donley, we're not down here begging. . . . All we're asking for is a chance. . . . At Trenholm we had our own basketball team, we had our own cheerleaders, we had our own student council. We came to Deshler and you had yours, your football team, your cheerleaders. Now we are not begging, all we're asking is to give us a chance to play football, to be cheerleaders," to be this, to be that. It was beautiful. That man [the principal] just sat there and said, "Wow! As far as I'm concerned, I'm going to give you a chance to do anything you want." And when they [the students] left . . . he sat and talked with me. I really think it changed his mind about a whole lot of things. . . . He had never had a Black child sit down and go over these things with him. (Morris & Morris, 2000a, p. 164)

For this White principal, Flora was the "unusual" African American student, not at all what he expected of ordinary African American students. After all, in Alabama in 1969, he had never experienced this kind of interaction with African American students. It seemed easy and perhaps logical for him and other educators like him to believe all the negative stereotypes about African American children who for decades attended the "other" high school across town. If Mr. Donley had spent time at Trenholm High School before it closed, as did African American educators and parents, he would have observed that the attributes exhibited by Flora were those expected of the usual African American student rather than the unusual.

African American students who attended Trenholm High School continued to experience the unusual Negro myth as they pursued degrees in desegregated colleges and universities. In 1963, Wendell Gunn enrolled at Florence State College (now the University of North Alabama), located six miles from Tuscumbia. In 1965, all students and faculty at Florence State College learned that Gunn was a high achiever when he received an award on Recognition Day. An article in the *Flora-Ala*, the college's student newspaper, noted that

> in 1963 when many American colleges were experiencing uneasy integration, Wendell Wilkie Gunn quietly enrolled at Florence State, entering the Junior Class. Two years later he received a standing ovation from his fellow students. The occasion was "Recognition Day," the annual spring program in the amphitheater in which FSU ceremoniously honors its outstanding students. In 1965 the Award to the Outstanding Student in Physics (highest average) went to Wendell Wilkie Gunn. When this announcement was made, the audience came to its feet, gratefully applauding the accomplishments of a young man who had broken the color barrier with grace as well as courage. ("First Black," 1972)

Wendell later remarked, "The first thing that somebody tried to say to me was well, you are an *unusual Negro*." He further stated: "I knew a lot of Negroes who were smarter than me . . . but who didn't have the same opportunities or strokes of luck that I did" (Morris & Morris, 2000a, p. 141). According to Wendell, he was not unusual at all—he exhibited attributes that were the expected norm for African American children in the Trenholm school community.

A related phrase that communicates the same myth is "acting White." Valerie recalled that her teenage daughter, Mona, was concerned because White classmates at her desegregated school accused her of acting White. In the course of their conversation, Valerie explained to Mona that being a good student, having good social skills, and treating people with kindness and respect were not color specific. These attributes were unrelated to race or color, but were related to socialization and individual choice. African American teenagers, in particular, may experience peer pressure from both African American and White classmates because they refuse to follow the stereotype of the expected or the usual myth that has been perpetuated about African American students in the community.

The myth of the unusual Negro was also accepted and acted on as teachers were placed in desegregated schools in Tuscumbia City Schools and other communities throughout the South. Rubie Leslie Buckingham, a graduate of Trenholm who taught in Tuscumbia schools for 42 years, remarked on what happened during those early years of desegregation (1965–1969):

They [the school board] got the teachers who had master's degrees [from Trenholm and Southside]. That means they took the highest qualified teachers first [for the previously all-white schools]. . . . Why are you going to take the best from me? I need some of the best. You should just mix it up. But they didn't do it. . . . They sent the inexperienced white teachers to Southside. Everything they sent us was right out of college, no experience. Yet they pulled the best that we had and took it over there." (Morris & Morris, 2000a, p. 156)

Valerie accepted a remedial reading teaching position at an African American school in a neighboring community in the late 1960s. Her principal proudly reported the success Valerie appeared to be having with her upper-elementary school students who had failed in past years to develop the appropriate reading skills. To test the effectiveness of the reading program that Valerie was using, the associate superintendent for curriculum administered a standardized reading test to Valerie's students at the beginning and at the end of a 6-week period. The pre/post test analysis revealed that the students showed unusual improvement in reading test scores. Then the decision was made by the central office that Valerie would teach reading at one of the White elementary schools the following summer. Valerie's principal's was also afraid that she would be assigned to teach at one of the White schools the next academic year because of the mounting pressure to desegregate faculties at all schools. Again, as was the case in Tuscumbia, African American teachers who were considered unusual Negroes, or what the central office considered the best, would be the first transferred to the all-White or predominately White schools. However, instead, Valerie chose to accept a permanent position as a reading teacher at a historically Black college that summer. Her African American principal, Mr. Ryan, was delighted that this "unusual" teacher would continue her work with African American students.

HAVE THINGS CHANGED?

In the last decade of the 20th century, the myth of the unusual Negro continued to prevail in communities throughout this nation. Veteran suburban White teachers in a school-university partnership in the mid-South continue to be "surprised" when they visit urban, predominately African American schools where the buildings are clean, the schools are orderly, students are actively engaged in educational tasks, and students are kind and respectful of their teachers and of other students.

Undergraduate students enrolled in a teacher preparation program at a large, predominately White urban university designed to equip them to teach in urban schools are required to complete field experiences in urban high-poverty schools. Students interview parents of children enrolled in urban schools and spend a specified number of hours observing and participating in urban classrooms with children. Pre-service students enrolled in this urban education course spent their observation/participation hours in two urban school buildings (on adjacent campuses) with predominately African American student bodies (grades K–8). At the end of the semester, students wrote reflective statements regarding their experiences. One white male student noted:

> My attitude was greatly affected [by interviews with parents of children enrolled in schools]. I had a negative attitude going into the interviews. I was under the idea that . . . City Schools' parents cared little about their child's education. I was wrong. All of my parents wanted to be involved. The methods for promoting involvement were not adequate. I want parents like this to be involved in my classroom. I will do everything in my ability to keep them involved.

A second student remarked: "This experience has definitely affected my attitude toward working in the urban school system. I have seen the need for caring, positive role models in the schools and feel that these children need teachers who really care about their education."

A third student was concerned about being a White teacher in a predominately African American school. It so happened that her observation/participation hours were spent in a classroom with all African American students who had a very effective White teacher. The pre-service teacher remarked:

> I have also become more comfortable with the idea of being a minority race in the classroom. I had wondered how a homogeneous group of children would react to a teacher of another race. I also wondered how the parents would feel toward having a Caucasian teacher. Through this experience, I have gained more confidence and the feeling that I would be accepted in an urban classroom.

A fourth student, who planned to teach second grade, wanted to be prepared to teach eighth-grade as well. So she chose to observe in an eighth grade classroom because with a K–8 certificate, she could be assigned any grade within that range as a new or veteran teacher. She stated:

> Working with these children [African American children] really showed me how much of an impact environment and family life have on children and their success in school. In the beginning I would have written these children off as just being "BAD." As I got to know them, my attitude changed a lot. This experience has made me more open-minded about working with children from urban environments. As a White, middle-class person, I really could not relate to the problems these children face. After working with the students at Baron Elementary School, I feel more willing to work with students from urban environments because they are just *ordinary* kids [emphasis added].

A fifth student realized that the African American children enrolled at the urban school wanted the same thing that all children want and need. She remarked:

> This experience greatly changed my attitudes toward children and their desires to learn. I came to realize that the children in this classroom wanted *active* learning; they wanted praise from the teacher; and they wanted to succeed in school. It is now my obligation as an educator to provide them with these opportunities, especially because many children are not currently receiving them.

The last student was an African American who appears to have spent limited (if any) time in low-income, predominately African American schools or communities in the city. She expressed her discomfort in being assigned to observe/participate in the school.

> I was really excited and at the same time anxious about getting the opportunity to observe actual classroom settings at an urban school. When I heard that it was Baron Elementary School, I thought to myself, "That's a bad neighborhood." Then I remembered from my experience with the parent interviews to dispel the notion of stereotypes. So I did. I was still a little uncomfortable about going to the school. I had *heard* that the school was lacking in some areas of resource. . . . When this assignment was completed, my philosophy of teaching had broadened. All children can learn, no matter what their background is. . . . Now I look forward to working with kids in

urban schools. They're no *different* from the others. . . . I believe there's no such thing as a "bad" student. [emphasis added]

Trenholm graduates indicated that their favorite teachers had high expectations of their students and were fair. They expected them to work hard and reminded them often that they had to be twice as good as Whites in order to get the same jobs. However, when African American students were high achievers at the desegregated school, their White teachers and classmates described them as "unusual Negroes." This was clear evidence to African American students, and their parents, that their White teachers had low expectations for them. Their White teachers did not expect them to be high academic achievers. However, the White community *did* have high expectations that African Americans students would help Deshler High School win football and basketball championships (Morris & Morris, 2000a).

The myths and stereotypes about African American children, their lives and learning, continue to prevail among veteran and pre-service teachers, both White and African American, especially among those who have had little or no interaction with these children and their families. And of course, they may have many experiences that will reinforce these myths. A belief in these myths can have devastating effects on the educational experiences of African American children. Such a belief gives license to teachers to limit their expectations of children's abilities and thus limit the educational opportunities provided for them in classroom and school environments. What if these myths were eliminated from the minds of educators and school policymakers in this country? What would be the process?

CHAPTER NINE

Conclusion: Lessons Learned About Schooling from the 20th Century

IN THIS FINAL chapter, we take a look at how selected lessons from the school stories of one small Northwest Alabama community are related to the unmet promises of school desegregation.

AMERICAN SCHOOLS AT THE CLOSE OF THE 20TH CENTURY

At the close of the 20th century, educators, along with professionals in many different fields of endeavor, attempted to identify the important developments in their fields over the past 100 years and to make predictions for the future. The schooling of American children has gone through a great number of changes during the 20th century. Some examples include:

- from education for a few to publicly financed, compulsory education for the masses
- from a few months of schooling per year to 9–12 months per year
- from teachers with little or no training to 16 years or more of required education and certification, including continuing professional development
- from one-room schoolhouses to large, comprehensive elementary, middle, and secondary schools
- from segregated schools, based on race, to desegregation, then resegregation, especially in large urban areas that have experienced White flight to the suburbs
- from neighborhood schools to busing for desegregation and magnet schools and return to a demand for small neighborhood schools
- use of technology—calculators, computers, CD-ROMS, video play-

ers, cameras, and other equipment—as an instructional tool in class-rooms and schools

- a return to home-schooling for many families who are dissatisfied with the values being taught and/or the perceived quality of education being provided in public schools
- demand by some citizens to use vouchers (from public funds) to pay for children's attendance at private and parochial schools that have been deemed of higher quality than selected public schools
- increased demand for accountability of public schools by communities through higher standards, higher expectations of students, and high-stakes testing
- use of whole-school reform models to improve academic achievement of students, especially in urban school districts where large numbers of students make low scores on standardized achievement tests

In *Lessons of a Century: A Nation's Schools Come of Age*, Reeves (2000) provided a brief overview of some of the most significant accomplishments of education during the 20th century. She stated that

> by any measure, the educational achievements of the past 100 years are heroic in scale: universal public schooling; broad-based access to college; the democratization of a melting-pot culture; and provision of the skills and wherewithal to power an economic miracle, win two world wars, land on the moon, and defeat Communism.
>
> But the story of 20th century education is not simple, linear progression to greatness. It is a tale of cycles of reform. A fitful journey of stops and starts through the social, political, and philosophical conundrums of a defining age. (p. 1)

While the events and accomplishments noted above summarize many of the changes that have affected the schooling of all children in this country, historical viewpoints like these often omit many significant experiences that are major milestones in the lives of African Americans and other citizens of color. The following is one attempt to begin to fill in some of those gaps of omission.

CHALLENGES AND OPPORTUNITIES FOR AMERICAN SCHOOLS IN THE 21ST CENTURY

Trenholm High School was a small African American high school that operated in Tuscumbia, Alabama, for more than 90 years. It was a 1–12 school until 1966, when a separate elementary school (1–6) was erected two blocks south of the building to serve the African American community. Many of the lessons learned from these school stories are relevant to the growing body of research related to the support of small schools in improving the academic achievement of African American children and other children of color in this country.

Lesson 1: African American communities provided a good education for their children long before the 1954 Brown decision and school desegregation. African American citizens in Tuscumbia established the Osborne Academy in 1877, which became the Tuscumbia Colored Public School in 1887 and Trenholm High School in 1921 (Morris & Morris, 2000a). The African American community in Tuscumbia was subject to "double taxation" to support their schools as were African Americans throughout the South (Anderson, 1988; Morris & Morris, 2000a; Walker, 1998).

African Americans in many southern communities established and operated their own schools, despite antiliteracy laws, before the missionary societies and the Freedmen's Bureau began their efforts following the Civil War (Anderson, 1988). Anderson reported that a Black school existed in Savannah, Georgia, from 1833 to 1865, unknown to the slave regime, under the direction of a Black woman named Deveaux. He further noted that when the northern missionaries and Freedmen's Bureau representatives arrived in the South following Emancipation, much to their surprise they found that many ex-slaves had organized and staffed their own educational collectives and schools and were unwilling to be controlled by the "civilized Yankees." A number of researchers have reported on the quality of segregated schools for African American children during the 20th century (Cecelski, 1994; Dempsey & Noblit, 1996; Edwards, 1996; Foster, 1997; Rodgers; 1975; Sowell, 1976; Walker, 1996).

Lesson 2: From the beginning of the 20th century, the majority of southern African American educators rejected the philosophy that the training of African Americans should be limited to industrial education. Despite the intense team efforts of northern philanthropists and southern planters, many elementary, secondary, and normal schools like Trenholm High refused to adopt the Hampton-Tuskegee model of industrial training, developed by Samuel Chapman Armstrong at Hampton, as its primary mode of education for African American children (Anderson, 1988; Morris & Morris, 2000a). For example, Jones (1969) reported that the secondary course of study at Trenholm High School in 1910 included English, mathematics, Latin, German, pedagogy and psychology, physics, biology, and history. His report also noted that sewing was the only industrial subject taught in the high school. In addition to sewing, the elementary students had shuck work and raffia (African palm tree leaves used for making mats and baskets). During the mid-fifties, a full course of vocational home economics and auto mechanics was added to the classical liberal curriculum and established as electives for Trenholm students. This curriculum pattern continued until the school was closed in 1969.

Anderson (1988) reported that the Hampton-Tuskegee curriculum had as its mission the training of common school teachers for the South's Black educational system, not the development of trade or technical skills. He further stated that

> the primary aim was to work the prospective teachers long and hard so that they would embody, accept, and preach an ethic of hard toil or the "dignity of labor." Then, and only then, believed Armstrong, could his normal school graduates develop the appropriate values and character to teach the children of the South's distinctive black laboring class. (p. 34)

This model was opposed by many African Americans, who viewed it as Armstrong intended: "the effective removal of black voters and politicians from southern political life, the relegation of black workers to the lowest forms of labor in the southern economy [farm workers and domestics], and the establishment of a general southern racial hierarchy" (p. 36).

Lesson 3: Relationships can mean everything in improving the academic achievement of African American children. In Chapter 5, Veronica, Erin, Manual, and Maria told stories that clearly demonstrated that Trenholm High School was a place where students felt like members of a family. In this small, segregated, neighborhood 1–12 school, the principals and the teachers knew the names of all of the students and the parents. Ifill-Lynch (1998) noted that "the principle of small schools, in which teachers and students know each other well, is good for all children" (p. 48).

Ark and Wagner (2000) revealed a commonality in the small high schools they visited in the Northeast; powerful relationships. They indicated that these schools were "designed around relationships: the relationships of the students to the work, the relationships between the students and the teachers, and the relationships among the adults in the school" (p. 50). And these schools boast nearly 100 percent completion and college-acceptance rates. Each of the schools they visited had fewer than 400 students. They reported that, like Trenholm High School in many ways,

> there is no anonymity in these schools. The principal knows every student. Every teacher knows his or her students. Collectively, they are tenacious about finding a way to reach *every student*. They are relent-

less about their expectations for quality work and college acceptance. Every student is connected to at least one adult who shares responsibility of helping that student navigate the system and prepare for further learning. There is no graffiti, no hostility, almost no violence, and an atmosphere of mutual respect and collaboration. (Ark & Wagner, 2000, p. 50; emphasis added)

Gladden (1998) reported that

research has found that school size affects social aspects of a school, which in turn, affects the level of student achievement. Thus, although school size may not directly affect student achievement, it may affect the environment of schools, and that environment affects student achievement. For example, small school size has been shown to affect students' involvement in school activities and student involvement in extracurricular activities is related to higher levels of achievement. Thus, changes in school size may not directly affect achievement, but they may raise student's participation in school life, which then raises their achievement. (p. 116)

These findings lead logically to Lesson 4, which is related to the promise of small schools in closing the achievement gap between Whites and African Americans and other children of color in this nation.

Lesson 4: Small schools offer great promise for promoting the academic achievement of African American children and other children of color. Small schools may be defined as follows:

- small size, preferable no more than 350 students in elementary schools, 500 students in high schools;
- cohesive, self-selected faculty;
- substantial autonomy;
- coherent curricular focus that provides continuous educational experience;
- inclusive admissions; and
- positive academic and behavioral change. (Fine, 1998, p. 3)

Gladden (1998) found that "students in small schools are suspended less often, feel safer at school, use drugs less often, and are truant from school less often than students in larger schools" (p. 113). He also reported that smaller schools, as compared with large schools, enabled minority students and students from low socioeconomic backgrounds to perform significantly better academically. Gladden noted that "in small schools, the relationship between teachers and administrative staff is more collegial than in large schools" (p. 144) and emphasized the relationship between positive school climate and improved academic achievement. These findings should be good news for policymakers and school personnel as they consider the kind of school structure and size that best meets the needs of students of color enrolled in our schools.

Lesson 5: The promises of equality of educational opportunities for African American children are not ensured merely by closing poorly equipped, segregated school buildings and allowing African American children to sit next to White children in well-equipped, desegregated, formerly all-white school buildings. Trenholm High School students reported that the top three factors in making their school a good school—that is, qualified, dedicated, and caring teachers, the range of school programs and activities, and parental and community support and involvement—were either threatened or eliminated when the students began attending the desegregated high school in their town. African American students no longer experienced the family environment that existed at Trenholm; they did not feel that sense of belonging. White teachers and students were hostile toward them and their parents, and rules were enforced that discouraged their active participation in extracurricular activities. It appeared that the cultural and racial biases of teachers were embedded in instructional and curricula practices. There was no PTA at Deshler, so parents were unable to be actively involved in the life of the school in ways in which they were accustomed (Morris & Morris, 2000a).

It appeared that the social and emotional losses of desegregation in this community had not been weighed as critical factors that affected academic achievement. This school community lost its buildings, which amounted to nearly 100 years of blood, sweat, and tears of hundreds of African Americans—teachers, principals, parents, and other community residents—who worked, struggled, and sacrificed to make Trenholm a good school for their children. This school community also lost their school colors, their symbols, and their mascot. All of these were important socially and emotionally to the students and to the African American community. It was around these symbols that the school community rallied (Morris & Morris, 2000a). All of these factors affected the ability of students to focus on academic tasks.

Peebles (2000) questioned whether the school desegregation issue is a resolvable one in this country. He wrote:

> Now, with the emphasis on quality schools in neighborhoods, the cause of desegregation has moved to the background. To predict the future of

school desegregation is hazardous. But has any other issue commanded more attention, stirred more emotions, and affected more people in our country? What other issue of the 20th century has taken longer to resolve? Is it resolvable? (p. 91).

Lesson 6: Teachers should be growing or they must be going. Irvine (1991) reported that "the most significant teacher variable associated with school success was the quality of the staff development and inservice programs" (p. 101). Teachers and principals at Trenholm High School were not only active participants in professional development activities to improve the academic achievement of their students, but were leaders in local, state, and national organizations devoted to that goal. Teachers at Trenholm appeared to be well qualified for the classes they were assigned to teach, as documented by the 1955 accreditation report (*Report*, 1955): "The committee commends the teaching staff and administration for having high school teachers with college degrees and having made teaching choices and assignments in relation to your major and minor fields of professional training with few exceptions" (p. 40).

George Washington Trenholm, the third principal at Trenholm High School, emphasized the importance of the professional development of teachers in his address delivered at the National Association of Teachers in Colored Schools in 1911. He stated that "teachers are constantly reminded that there must be some growing or there will be some going" (Trenholm, c. 1911, p. 1). White teachers and administrators at Deshler High School did not appear to have had the professional-development training needed to work effectively with their new students—African Americans from Trenholm. They needed training much like that described by Kuglemass (2000) for teachers at Besty Miller:

> Teachers at Betsy Miller participated in race relations workshops designed to help them examine their own racism. They also began investigating how cultural biases were embedded in instructional and assessment practices. They set out to counteract racism by implementing instructional methods that strengthened the identity, pride, and performance of African American children. (p. 26)

These instructional practices were in place at Trenholm but not at Deshler. Ifill-Lynch (1998) reminded us that teachers must be scholars no matter whom they teach.

As knowledge changes and new reforms are developed, schools are constantly searching for ways to increase academic achievement in schools in all communities. In order to maintain high standards and a rigorous curriculum for the children in our care, teachers must be active members of the learning community in their school and district. Ifill-Lynch (1998) stated:

> I think that sometimes in small schools, you can get so busy with relationships that you forget the rigor that you're teaching. The fact remains that children learn all the time, so we're always on. I think it's part of the role. And do you know how you keep on the rigor? You remind yourself constantly." (p. 49)

The professional development of teachers needs to be specific and focused on the needs of children in their school and classrooms. Morris and Chance (1997) refer to this type of training as "customized professional development." This kind of professional development should be tied to the school-improvement plan for a specific building with the activities being conducted on site and often through demonstrations, observations, and feedback in specific classrooms. The continuing professional development of teachers and of principals is essential if we are to improve student achievement (Sarason, 1993).

Lesson 7: Effective schools require the active engagement of a community of learners in the educational activities of the school. Segregated African American schools like Trenholm High School could not have operated effectively without the active involvement of families and community residents. Yet when African Americans began attending Deshler High School, structures were eliminated that had offered opportunities for parents to be active participants in the life of the school in helpful and positive ways.

Research studies conducted during the last half of the 20th century demonstrated that family involvement in the life of the school can contribute to positive educational outcomes for children (Arvizu, 1996; Bauch, 1988; Becher, 1986; Chavkin, 1993; Davies, 1988; Hoover-Dempsey, Bassler, & Brissie, 1992; Mager, 1980; Moles, 1993; Powell, 1989). Despite the obstacles of limited skills and knowledge among teachers and parents, of restricted opportunities for interaction, and of psychological and cultural barriers (Moles, 1993), with appropriate professional development, school personnel and families can work together to plan effective family involvement programs (Morris & Taylor, 1997).

Hoerr (2000) emphasized the need for a variety of stakeholders to be active in the life of the schools. He noted that "good schools are communities of learners, many younger and some older, but all learning with and from one another. In good schools, learners of all ages create knowledge and gain understanding" (p. 44).

Lesson 8: The myth of the "unusual Negro" continued to permeate the belief system of many White Americans at the end of 20th century. In Chapter 8, Valerie, Maria, and Wendell related their "unusual Negro" stories. Because they were intelligent, articulate, hard-working, high achievers who had good social skills and high career aspirations, they were considered unusual, a novelty, or "acting White" by their White peers and teachers. Whites seemed surprised when African American students exhibited these positive characteristics. In the Trenholm High School community in Tuscumbia, this was the "usual" behavior expected of African American students. These were the values and ideals that were communicated and reinforced by parents, teachers, and other community residents in this African American community, and in African American communities throughout this country.

At the end of the century, this myth of the unusual Negro still prevailed in some segments of society. Pre-service and veteran teachers involved in a school-university partnership at a large urban university were surprised to find orderly environments and children attending tenaciously to academic tasks in schools with predominately African American enrollments. Ladson-Billings (1994) suggested two strategies that may be useful in helping to eradicate this myth/stereotype of the unusual Negro in educational settings: (1) pre-service teachers should have early, systematic, and prolonged immersion experiences in African American culture and (2) administrators should select teachers who are willing and committed to teaching in schools with large numbers of African American children, rather than placing teachers in these settings because they are lowest on the seniority list. In addition, teachers need to be keen observers of their students and get to know them as individuals—and know their families as well (Morris & Morris, 2000a).

Resegregation of African Americans and Whites in schools and other settings will only provide fuel allowing myths like the unusual Negro to persist. In order to prepare teachers and principals to work effectively with African Americans and other children of color in our schools, many teacher education programs must change the way they prepare these professionals for careers in K–12 schools.

Lesson 9: The characteristics of race, ethnicity, religion, gender, disability, place of residence, and socioeconomic background of family must cease to be criteria used to deny children in this country the right to an effective and equitable education. This country can no longer afford to squander its human resources based on physical characteristics. The leadership potential and other skills of all its citizens are needed. We must not allow stereotypes, biases, or pre-judgments to dictate or define the ability or potential of children based on skin color, economic background, or perceived or actual disability.

At the close of the 20th century, while manifesting itself in much more subtle ways than earlier, race continued to be a major problem that affected people of color in negative ways in every aspect of their lives—educationally, politically, economically, and socially. Marian Wright Edelman (1999) stated so eloquently what happens to children of color and other children in this country who are considered by the majority to be different in some way:

> In our nation and world, White children have been assigned more value as a group than Black and Brown and Asian and Native American children. Affluent children are accorded more respect and resources than children who are poor and need them more. Children in single-parent families or born to teen parents are assigned the stigma we often attach to the parents they did not choose. Children with special physical, mental, or emotional needs are sometimes shunned and made the butt of jokes and jeers. Girls as a group face many barriers that boys do not in a world still characterized more by male privilege than by gender equality and mutual respect. Some boys—especially Black boys—are accorded no respect and are expected to control their rage from unequal treatment without crying or protesting—legally or illegally. (p. 134)

Lesson 10: What we need most to improve academic achievement in America is a caring, competent, and qualified teacher in every classroom. Graduates of Trenholm High School identified caring, competent, and committed teachers as the most important factor making their school a good school. While the attribute of caring is mentioned often in recent teacher education literature (Dempsey & Noblit, 1993; Foster, 1997; Irvine, 1991; Ladson-Billings, 1994; Noddings, 1992; Report, 1996; Thousand & Villa, 1995; Traina, 1999; Walker, 1996), the primary focus of reforms in teacher-preparation programs appears to be on the other two Cs—competence and commitment. This teacher attribute of caring is related to the issue of inclusion. As we move into the new millennium, a culturally responsive teaching force is needed to provide effective teachers for all children in our classrooms. Teachers must be able to connect with learners regardless of racial, ethnic, social, and behavioral characteristics (Thousand & Villa, 1995). When students trust their teachers and have established a caring relationship with them, students are more likely to care about what teachers want them to learn (Morris, Taylor, & Wilson, 2000).

We need teachers in schools who are competent to meet the needs of the children who come through their doors, whoever they are and at whatever developmental level they happen to be. Edelman (1999) agrees that children go to school ready to learn and full of joy and laughter until they are discouraged because they don't already know all the things teachers think they ought to know. Children are expected to be ready for the curriculum we have designed, rather than our designing curricula to meet the needs of the children who enter our classrooms and schools. And because of this lack of congruency, children are too often demeaned and stigmatized by low expectations, unjust labels, and mistreatment by adults in the school environment. Teachers blame the teachers before them for all the problems that children bring to the classroom and everyone blames the parents—even after children have been in school for several years. As early as kindergarten, teachers and other school personnel contribute to their young eager charges' becoming potential dropouts and candidates for juvenile detention centers and prisons as adults.

Edelman's (1999) query reminds us to live up to our commitment to equality of educational opportunity for all of our children. She states:

> Is it fair that poor children in the poorest neighborhoods have the poorest schools, the poorest prepared teachers, the poorest equipment, the poorest school buildings, libraries, laboratories, the fewest computers, counselors, school nurses, and enrichment programs and the lowest expectations by teachers, and a public that blames them for achieving poorly on the tests for which we have not prepared them? (p. 149)

And how do we retain good teachers once we have found them—especially in high-poverty schools with large enrollments of African Americans and other children of color? A number of writers have made suggestions that are worthy of consideration by policymakers and school personnel (Ascher, 1991; Crosby, 1999; Gordon, 1999; Horn, 1999; Jackson, 1999; Report 1996). Several of these major strategies are described here:

- Teachers deserve a highly qualified principal who understands teaching and learning for adults *and* children, just as students deserve a qualified teacher. The principal, who should come from the ranks of highly skilled teachers, is the instructional leader for the school and seeks opportunities and resources within and outside the school building to support teachers in meeting the achievement needs of the students (Report, 1996; Sarason, 1993; Teachers Take Charge, 1996; When School Leaders, 2000). Barth (1990) indicated that "when the central office runs a service agency for principals, then principals are able to set up service agencies for teachers, and teachers for children. The chain of command can then become a chain of support" (cited in Holcomb, 1999, p. 118).

- Reward good teachers who are willing to teach in high-poverty schools with good pay, ample supplies and equipment, good physical plants, and the continuing high-quality professional development that is required to support the high academic achievement of the children they teach (Ascher, 1991; Crosby, 1999; Gordon, 1999; Horn, 1999; Jackson, 1999; Report, 1996).
- Reward good teaching by paying good master teachers well to remain in the classroom and in schools to mentor novice teachers—for at least 3 years—and struggling veteran teachers. Being promoted to a supervisory or administrative position should not be the *only* reward for good teaching. (Ascher, 1991; Report, 1996; "When School Leaders," 2000).
- Discontinue the practice of "demoting" poorly performing administrators *back* to the classroom. This practice devalues the role of teacher, the role of the person who is on the front lines everyday, working with the most important persons in our schools—the children. This practice suggests that one can be incompetent at "really important jobs" in the school or district, but anyone can teach. Is this the message we want to send to our children and school community?
- Commit a considerable portion of the human resources now designated as central office staff to provide support to teachers at the school and classroom levels. Rather than being evaluators almost *exclusively*, these highly trained, seasoned professionals may best assist in improving the academic achievement of children if they are assigned to specific buildings where they provide support, demonstrations, coaching, and feedback on a daily basis at the classroom level (Report, 1996; Sarason, 1993; Teachers Take Charge, 1996).

Good teachers are critical in helping to develop high-quality scientists, doctors, businesspeople, lawyers, nurses, social workers, carpenters, musicians, artists, and all the other professionals and skilled workers who are needed to continue to make this country great as it helps all its citizens to enjoy a good quality of life and share its good fortunes with peoples of the world.

WORK YET TO BE DONE

In summary, what was lost at Trenholm were some of the qualities that communities throughout this country are seeking today—that is, small neighborhood schools that have strong leadership; qualified and caring teachers; a safe, orderly, and positive environment; a wide range of co-curricular activities in which *all* students are encouraged to participate; and the active involvement and support of families and the community. The desegregated school had a superior physical plant, a wide range of course offerings, and ample instructional supplies and equipment. These were the gains, but made at a substantial cost.

McCready (1996) agrees that African Americans in other southern communities and in northern cities suffered losses similar to those of the Trenholm school community with desegregation. He stated:

> First, integration took its greatest toll on African-American children by requiring that they attend schools outside their home environments. Amid predominately white teachers and students, pupil-teacher relationships were strained for African American students. Second, massive firings or reassignments of African American teachers, principals, and administrators diluted the number of African-American personnel in control of curriculum. Third, as the traditional education role of African-American parents was dismantled, many were unsure how to interact with the predominately white school system. These events in effect robbed African Americans of the community control they had enjoyed historically. (p. 111)

There is no doubt that as a whole, African Americans in this country are better off educationally than they were at the beginning of the 20th century. "Yet scholars and educators disagree over how much of their gains can be attributed to desegregation. And as the stubborn achievement gap between black and white students underscores, in many respects they still have a long way to go" (Hendrie, 2000, p. 73). However, some researchers believe that as a country we have taken some steps backward. "In American race relations, the bridge from the 20th century may be leading back into the 19th century," warned a 1997 report on school resegregation by the Harvard Project on School Desegregation headed by Orfield. There is no evidence that separate but equal works any more than it did a century ago" (in Hendrie, 2000, p. 73).

Despite the progress made in civil rights especially during the last half of the 20th century, inequities still abound in public education and in other segments of our society. At the beginning of a new century, race and class still matter (Fine, 2000; Hendrie, 2000; Ingersoll, 2001; McNeil, 2000; Wolk, 2000). Some critics will say, that was then (before desegregation), and this is now. And we say to them, look carefully around your community and other towns and cities throughout this country. Inequities in educational opportunities continue to exist. And you may discover, as many others have, that in many instances *then is also now.*

School reform that includes the standards movement, accountability, and high-stakes testing, as presently conceived and implemented, may be contributing to the continuing inequities in public education. Wolk (2000) reported that the most egregious omission from the standards movement is the opportunity-to-learn standard. He states that "for students to have a reasonable opportunity to learn, they need qualified teachers, a coherent and rigorous curriculum, safe and orderly schools in good repair, supplies and equipment to enhance teaching and learning" (p. 14). Studies continue to show that African Americans and other children of color are more likely to be enrolled in schools where these attributes are not in place, just as they were not *before* the 1954 *Brown* decision (Ascher, 1991; Hendrie, 2000; Ingersoll, 2001; McNeil, 2000; Wolk, 2000).

Ingersoll (2001) asserted that the high-stakes testing that takes place in states like Texas actually creates new inequalities for poor and minority students rather than eliminating inequalities as intended. She stated that

> the testing of students increasingly drives curriculum and compromises both teaching and the role of the student in learning. This prescriptive teaching creates a new form of discrimination as teaching to the fragmented and narrow information on the test comes to substitute for a substantive curriculum in the schools of poor and minority youths. Disaggregating school-level scores by children's race appears to be an attempt to promote equity, but the high stakes attached to the scores have made many schools replace the regular curriculum in minority students' classrooms with test-prep materials that have virtually no value beyond practicing for the tests. The scores go up in these classrooms, but academic quality goes down. The result is a growing inequality between the content and quality of education provided to white, middle-class children and that provided to those in poor and minority schools. (p. 730)

In some urban schools with a majority of poor African Americans enrolled, students no longer have outside play each day, or an enriching social studies curriculum or the co-curricular activities that can contribute to increased academic achievement. School officials, as noted by Ingersoll (2001), mandate that the majority of time must be spent on test-prep activities, which is most often reading and mathematics—whatever subjects are included on standardized state tests that are used as the single measure for district-, school-, and classroom-level accountability. Schools with more affluent students whose scores are already "up" are not held to these narrow curriculum standards.

Fine (2000) agreed with Trenholm (1912) about the high cost of refusing to get our act together in public education, particularly for children of color. She reported findings from a report called *And Justice for Some*:

The report talks to us about the criminalization of, particularly, African-American and Latino youth, telling us that 26 percent of young people who are arrested are African American. . . . Forty-four percent of African American youth who are arrested are detained; substantially fewer white youth are. Forty-six percent of African American juveniles go on to criminal court, while a majority of white juveniles get deferred to either juvenile court or alternatives. And 58 percent of the youth in state adult prisons are African American, more than doubling the proportion of those who are arrested. (Fine, 2000, p. 1)

There are other consequences of which we can be assured if we continue in the 21st century to be delinquent in carrying out our stated commitment of equal educational opportunities for all children in this country. We can be certain that we will have

- a surplus of citizens eligible for low-paying, poverty-level, unskilled and semi-skilled jobs and a lack of workers needed for skilled and professional positions;
- increased numbers of families who will be eligible for welfare and concomitant benefits such as health care;
- increasingly crowded court dockets in juvenile and adult criminal courts;
- the continuing need to build prisons and juvenile detention facilities—already a major public and private industry in this country; and
- fewer workers to keep the social security system afloat for those of us who are presently in the work force.

Jane Walters (2001), former commissioner of education for the State of Tennessee, communicated clearly and succinctly the rationale for providing a quality education for all of our children:

Our lives are inextricably intertwined with other people's children . . . . You are going to eat in restaurants where the food is prepared by other people's children. You're going to drive in cars built by other people's children. If you go to the airport and fly, the chance of your own child piloting that plane is infinitesimal. So you are going to put your life in the hands of other people's children. And in Memphis as in every other community, most of us are going to end our days in hospitals and nursing homes run by other people's children. And if those children have not had adequate education, all our lives are going to suffer.

These are just a few of the expected adverse consequences of refusing to work together as a nation to use the human, social, financial, and technological resources already available in this country to provide high-quality schooling for all children in all our communities. We have the resources and the know-how or the wisdom. The question is: Do we have the will— the strength of character—to use the resources to do the "right thing"?

References

African American History: Mary McLeod Bethune. (1999). [Online]. Available: *http://www.triadntr.net/~rdavis/bethune.htm*.

Alabamian and Times. (1870, May 5).

American Star, The. (1901a, May 29). Montgomery, AL: Alabama Department of Archives and History.

American Star, The. (1901b, June 12). Montgomery, AL: Alabama Department of Archives and History.

American Star, The. (1901c, November 28). Montgomery, AL: Alabama Department of Archives and History.

American Star, The. (1901d, December 12). Montgomery, AL: Alabama Department of Archives and History.

Anderson, J. D. (1988). *The education of blacks in the South, 1860–1935*. Chapel Hill: The University of North Carolina Press.

Ark, V. T., & Wagner, T. (2000). Between hope and despair: The case for smaller high schools. *Education Week, XIX*(41), 50, 76.

Arvizu, S. F. (1996). Family, community, and school collaboration. In J. Sikula (Ed.), *Handbook of research on teacher education* (pp. 814–819). New York: Simon & Schuster Macmillan.

Ascher, C. (1991). Retaining good teachers in urban schools. [Online]. *http://eric-web.tc.columbia.edu/digests/dig77.html*.

Barth, R. (1990). *Improving schools from within: Teachers, parents and principals can make the difference*. San Francisco: Jossey-Bass.

Bauch, P. (1988). Is parent involvement different in private schools? *Educational Horizons, 66*(2), 78–82.

Becher, R. (1986). Parent involvement: A review of research and principles of successful practice. In L. Katz (Ed.), *Current topics in early childhood education* (pp. 85–122). Norwood, NJ: Ablex Publishers.

Bergstrom, J. M., & O'Brien, L. A. (2001). Themes of discovery. *Educational Leadership, 58*(7), 29–33.

Board minutes: Tuscumbia city board of education. (1907, May 17).

Board minutes: Tuscumbia city board of education. (1944, October 19).

Board minutes: Tuscumbia city board of education. (1950, August 28).

Board minutes: Tuscumbia city board of education. (1955, January 31).

Brief and special mention. (1906, March 1). *The American Star*, p. 1. Montgomery, AL: Alabama Department of Archives and History.

Cecelski, D. (1994). *Along freedom road: Hyde County, North Carolina, and the fate of Black schools in the South*. Chapel Hill, NC: University of North Carolina Press.

Chavkin, N. (1993). Introduction: Families and the schools. In N. Chavkin (Ed.), *Families and schools in a pluralistic society* (pp. 1–17). Albany, NY: State University Press.

The city school closed. (1902, May 22). *The American Star*. Montgomery, AL: Alabama Department of Archives and History.

Coasters. (1999). *Charlie Brown*. [Online]. Available: *http://www.summer.com.br/ ~pfilho/html/lyrics/c/charlie_brown.txt*.

Colbert county deed record F. (1881, February 5), 553.

Colored city high school. (1905, December 12). *The Weekly Dispatch*.

Councill, W. H. (1901). *Address to the White people of Alabama*. Washington, DC: Howard University, Moorland-Spingarn Research Center.

Crosby, E. A. (1999). Urban schools forced to fail. *Phi Delta Kappan, 81*(4), 298–303.

Davies, D. (1988). Benefits and barriers to parent involvement. *Community Education Research Digest, 2*, 11–19.

Democrat, The. (1880, October 2).

Democrat, The. (1881, June 1).

Dempsey, V., & Noblit, G. (1993). The demise of caring in an African American community: One consequence of school desegregation. *The Urban Review, 25*(1), 47–61.

Dempsey, V., & Noblit, G. (1996). Cultural ignorance and school desegregation: A community narrative. In M. J. Shujaa (Ed.), *Beyond desegregation: The politics in African American schooling* (pp. 115–137). Thousand Oaks, CA: Corwin Press, Inc.

Desegregation of Tuscumbia Schools. (n.d.). Tuscumbia, AL: Tuscumbia City Schools.

Desegregation Plan for Tuscumbia City Schools. (1970, January 13). Submitted by Jack H. Vardaman, Superintendent, in a letter to The Honorable Frank M. Johnson, Jr., United District Judge, United States District Court, Montgomery, AL. Letter provided by Tuscumbia City Schools, Tuscumbia, AL.

Du Bois, W. E. B. (1989). *The souls of Black folk*. New York: Penguin Books. (Original work published 1903)

Edelman, M. W. (1999). *Lanterns: A memoir of mentors*. Boston: Beacon Press.

Edwards, P. A. (1996). Before and after school desegregation: African American parents' involvement in schools. In M. J. Shujaa (Ed.), *Beyond desegregation: The politics in African American schooling* (pp. 138–161). Thousand Oaks, CA: Corwin Press, Inc.

Fine, M. (1998). Introduction: What's so good about small schools? In M. Fine and J. I. Somerville (Eds.), *Small schools big imaginations: A creative look at urban public schools* (pp. 2–13). Chicago: Cross City Campaign for Urban School Reform.

Fine, M. (2000). The politics of urgency. [Online]. Available: *http://www.crosscity.org/ reports/mfine_paper1.htm*

First Black graduates to a standing ovation. (1972, December 3). *The Flora Ala*.

Fleming, W. L. (1905). Civil war and reconstruction in Alabama. New York: Columbia University Press.

Foster, M. (1997). *Black teachers on teaching*. New York: The New Press.

George Washington Carver. (1999a). [Online]. Available: *http://www.triadntr.net ~rdavis/carver.htm.*

George Washington Carver. (1999b). [Online]. Available: *http://www.ai.mit.edu/ ~edu~isbell/HFh/black/events_and_people/htm/004.g_w_carver.htnl*

Gladden, R. (1998). The small school movement: A review of the literature. In M. Fine and J. I. Somerville (Eds.), *Small schools big imaginations: A creative look at urban public schools* (pp. 113–131). Chicago: Cross City Campaign for Urban School Reform.

Gordon, G. L. (1999). Teacher talent and urban schools. *Phi Delta Kappan, 81*(4), 292–297.

Griaule, M., & Dieterlan, G. (1986). *The Pale Fox*. Chino Valley, Arizona, Continuum Foundation. P.O. Box 636, Chino Valley, Arizona 86323. (Original work published 1965)

Hamilton, C. (2000). Race and education: A search for legitimacy. *Harvard Educational Review, 38*(4), 669–684.

Hendrie, C. (2000). In black and white. In Education Week Staff, *Lessons of a century: A nation's schools come of age* (pp. 62–74). Bethesda, MD: Editorial Projects in Education.

High school notes. (1908a, April). *The American Star*. Alabama Department of Archives and History, Montgomery, AL.

High school notes. (1908b, May). *The American Star*. Alabama Department of Archives and History, Montgomery, AL.

Hilliard, A. G. (1997). *SBA: The reawakening of the African mind*. Gainesville, FL: Makare Publishing.

Hoerr, T. (2000). Doing things right, or doing right things: There's no checklist for leadership. *Education Week, XIX*(35), 44, 47.

Holcomb, E. L. (1999). *Getting excited about data: How to combine people, passion, and proof*. Thousand Oaks, CA: Corwin Press, Inc.

Horn, R. V. (1999). Inner-city schools: A multiple-variable discussion. *Phi Delta Kappan, 81*(4), 291–297.

Hoover-Dempsey, K., Bassler, O., & Brissie, J. (1992). Explorations in parent-school relations. *Journal of Educational Research, 85*(5), 287–294.

Ifill-Lynch, O. (1998). Perspectives: Administrators. In M. Fine and J. I. Somerville (Eds.), *Small schools big imaginations: A creative look at urban public schools* (pp. 44–52). Chicago: Cross City Campaign for Urban School Reform.

Ingersoll, R. M. (2001). The realities of out-of-field teaching. *Educational Leadership, 58*(8), 42–45.

Irvine, J. J. (1991). *Black students and school failure: Policies, practices, and prescriptions*. New York: Praeger.

Jackson, J. F. (1999). What are the real risk factors for African American children? *Phi Delta Kappan, 81*(4), 308–312.

Jones, J. T. (1969). *Negro education: A study of the private and higher schools for colored people in the United States*. New York: Arno Press and the New York Times.

Kozol, J. (1991). *Savage inequalities: Children in America's schools*. New York: Crown Publishers, Inc.

Kuglemass, J. W. (2000). Not made for defeat. *Educational Leadership, 57*(7), 25–28.

Ladson-Billings, G. (1994). *The dreamkeepers: Successful teachers of African American children.* San Francisco: Jossey-Bass.

Lanker, B. (1999). *I dream a world: Portraits of Black women who changed America.* New York: Stewart, Tabori & Chang.

Leftwich, N. (1935). *Two hundred years at Muscle Shoals.* Birmingham, AL: Multigraphic Advertising Co.

Long, W. M. (1981). Personal Interview. Tuscumbia, AL.

Mager, G. (1980). The conditions which influence teachers in initiating contacts with parents. *Journal of Educational Research, 73,* 276–282.

McCready, L. (1996). African Americans and community control of schools. In F. C. Jones-Wilson, C. A. Asbury, M. Okazawa-Rey, D. K. Anderson, S. M. Jacobs, & M. Fultz (Eds.), *Encyclopedia of African-American education* (pp. 109–113). Westport, CT: Greenwood Press.

McLaughlin, M. W. (2001). Community counts. *Educational Leadership, 58*(7), 14–18.

McNeil, L. M. (2000). Creating new inequalities: Contraditions of reform. *Phi Delta Kappan, 81*(10), 728–734.

Memorial tribute to its fourth president: George Washington Trenholm. (1950, August 3). The Alabama State College for Negroes, Montgomery, AL. Washington, DC: Howard University.

Memorial tribute to the fourth of the five presidents of Alabama State College: George Washington Trenholm. (1957, December 13). Alabama State College, Montgomery, AL. Washington, DC: Howard University.

Miller, B. M. (2001). The promise of after-school programs. *Educational Leadership, 58*(7), 6–12.

Moles, O. (1993). Collaboration between schools and disadvantaged parents: Obstacles and openings. In N. Chavkin (Ed.), *Families and schools in a pluralistic society* (pp. 21–49). Albany, NY: State University Press.

Morris, V. G. (1993, July). The closing of Trenholm High School: Was the baby thrown out with the bath water? Keynote address made at the Second Annual Reunion Banquet of Trenholm High School, Tuscumbia, AL.

Morris, V. G. (2000, December). Educating the Black child. Presentation made at the Annual Conference of the Office of Minority Health sponsored by the University of Memphis and the State of Tennessee Department of Health, Memphis, TN.

Morris, V. G., & Chance, L. (1997). Customized professional development for inservice teachers in a school-university partnership. *British Journal of Inservice Education, 23*(3), 335–348.

Morris, V. G., & Morris, C. L. (1981). The beginning of Black public education in Tuscumbia. *Journal of Muscle Shoals History, 9,* 66–73.

Morris, V. G., & Morris, C. L. (1993, July). Osborne Colored Academy: The forerunner of Trenholm High School? *Reflections of Trenholm High School Reunion 1993,* Tuscumbia, AL.

Morris, V. G., & Morris, C. L. (1995). Early schooling for Blacks in Tuscumbia, 1977–

1896: Before the arrival of George Washington Trenholm. *Journal of Muscle Shoals History, 14,* 82–90.

Morris, V. G., & Morris, C. L. (2000a). *Creating caring and nurturing educational environments for African American children.* Westport, CT: Bergin & Garvey, an imprint of Greenwood Publishing Group, Inc.

Morris, V. G., & Morris, C. L. (2000b, September). The teachers our children need: Lessons learned from a segregated African American community. Presentation made at the National Conference on Civil/Human Rights of Africanans, Memphis, TN.

Morris, V. G., & Morris. C. L. (2002). No more cotton picking: African American voices from a small southern town. In G. S. Boutte (Ed.). *School experiences of people from diverse ethnic backgounds* (pp. 17–42). Needham Heights, MA: Allyn & Bacon.

Morris, V. G., Morris, C. L, & Taylor, S. I. (1998, April). We did it once, can we do it again? Creating caring and nurturing educational environments for African American children. Paper presented at the 1998 Annual Meeting of the American Educational Research Association, San Diego, CA.

Morris, V. G., & Taylor, S. I. (1997). Alleviating barriers to family involvement in education: The role of teacher education. *Teaching and Teacher Education, 14*(2), 1–13.

Morris, V. G., Taylor, S. I., & Wilson, J. T. (2000). Using children's stories to promote peace in classrooms. *Early Childhood Education Journal, 28*(1), 46–54.

Morrison, R. D. (1994). *History of Alabama A & M University, 1875–1992.* Huntsville, AL: The Golden Rule Printers.

The Negro's last good opportunity to secure good, cheap homes: Segregation of the Negro. (1906, October 1). *The American Star.* Montgomery, AL: Alabama Department of Archives and History.

Noddings, N. (1992). *The challenge to care in schools: An alternative approach to education.* New York: Teachers College Press.

North Alabamian. (1889, July 19).

North Alabamian. (1896, September 11).

Pearce, J. C. (1977). *Magical child.* New York: E. P. Dutton.

Peebles, R. W. (2000). Desegregation and the "American dilemma." In Staff of Education Week, *Lessons of a century: A nation's schools come of age* (pp. 89–91). Bethesda, MD: Author.

Powell, D. (1989). *Families and early childhood education.* Washington, DC: National Association for the Education of Young Children.

Reeves, S. (2000). Introduction. In Staff of Education Week, *Lessons of a century: A nation's schools come of age* (p. 1). Bethesda, MD: Author.

Report of the National Commission on Teaching & America's Future. (1996). *What matters most: Teaching for America's future.* Woodbridge, VA: Author.

Report of visiting committee on evaluative criteria of Trenholm high school. (1955). Tuscumbia, AL: Author.

Rodgers, F. A. (1975). *The Black high school and its community.* Lexington, MA: Lexington Books, D. C. Heath and Company.

Sarason, S. B. (1993). *The case for change: Rethinking the preparation of educators.* San Francisco: Jossey-Bass.

Scarf drill, A, (1909, December). *The American Star*. Alabama Department of Archives and History, Montgomery, AL.

Sheeler, J. R. (1945, October). George Washington Trenholm. *The Negro History Bulletin*, pp. 17–20.

Sheridan, R. C. (1997, March 6). Carver's visit attracted large crowd locally. *Times Daily*, p. 1C.

Shoals life: Tuscumbia. (1998). Times Daily. [Online]. Available: *http://www.times daily.com/tuscumb.html*.

Sowell, T. (1976). Patterns of Black excellence. *Public Interest, 43*, 26–58.

Teachers take charge of their learning. (1996). Washington, DC: National Foundation for the Improvement of Education. [Online]. Available: *http://www.nfie.org/exec.htm*.

Thanks for the memories. (1981, May 20). *The Shoals News-Leader*, p. 4.

Thompson, T. T. (1925, October 17). Letter written by T. T. Thompson, Principal of Colored Public School, Demopolis, AL, to Dr. J. W. Abercrombie, State Superintendent of Education, Montgomery, AL. Washington, DC: Howard University, Moorland-Spingarn Research Center.

Thousand, J. S., & Villa, R. A. (1995). Managing complex change toward inclusive schooling. In R. A. Villa & J. S. Thousand (Eds.), *Creating an inclusive school* (pp. 51–79). Alexandria, VA: Association for Supervision and Development.

Traina, R. P. (1999). What makes a good teacher? *Education Week, XVIII*(19), 34.

Trenholm, G. W. (c., 1911). *Concentration on public high schools in the South rather than multiplying private secondary schools*. Address delivered at the National Association of Teachers in Colored Schools, St. Louis, MO. Washington, DC: Howard University, Moorland-Spingarn Research Center.

Trenholm, G. W. (1912, April 4). *Status of Negro education in Alabama*. Annual address of G. W. Trenholm, President of the Alabama Teachers' Association, delivered at Selma, AL. Washington, DC: Howard University, Moorland-Spingarn Research Center.

Tuscumbia, Alabama. (1878, May 3). *North Alabamian*.

Tuscumbia Dispatch, The. (1905, December 23).

Walker, V. S. (1996). *Their highest potential: African American school community in the segregated South*. Chapel Hill, NC: The University of North Carolina Press.

Walker, V. S. (1998). Focus on diversity. *Briefs, Newsletter of the American Association of Colleges for Teacher Education, 19*(12), 4–5, 8.

Walters, J. (2001, May 24). Kids count: Classroom at a Crosswords [video]. WREG-TV, Memphis, TN.

Webber, T. L. (1978). *Deep like the rivers: Education in the slave quarter communities, 1831–1865*. New York: W. W. Norton.

Weekly Dispatch, The. (1887, October 25).

Weekly Dispatch, The. (1888, June 19).

Weekly Dispatch, The. (1898, May 26).

Weekly Dispatch, The. (1901, July 25).

When school leaders support new teachers, everybody wins. (2000). *Education Update, 42*(5), 1, 6–7.

Wolk, R. (2000). Changing urban schools. [Online]. Available: *http://www.cross city.org/reports/chg_urb_hs.htm*.

Woodson, C. G. (1992). *The mis-education of the Negro*. Newport News, VA: United Brothers & Sisters Graphics & Printing. (Original work published 1933)

A word about our club. (1908, April). *The American Star*. Montgomery, AL: Alabama Department of Archives and History.

Yarbrough, T. E. (1981). *Judge Frank Johnson and human rights in Alabama*. University: University of Alabama Press.

Index

Note: Italicized page numbers refer to photographs.

About the Authors

Vivian Gunn Morris is Professor of Education in the Department of Instruction and Curriculum Leadership at the University of Memphis. She received a Ph.D. at Peabody College, Vanderbilt University, and master's and bachelor's degrees from Alabama A & M University. She was a faculty member at Community College of Philadelphia, Montclair State University, and Alabama A & M University. Dr. Morris has also taught at the preschool, elementary, junior high, and high school levels. Her numerous publications have appeared as articles, book chapters, and books. Dr. Morris's research, writing, and consultant interests include educating African American children, family involvement in education, urban education, professional development schools, and early childhood education. She was a recipient of the 1997 Association of Teacher Educators' Distinguished Research Award in Teacher Education for her research on family involvement in education. A recent book she co-authored with Curtis Morris, *Creating Caring and Nurturing Educational Environments for African American Children* (2000), was a finalist for the 2001 American Association of Colleges for Teacher Education's Book Award in Teacher Education.

Curtis L. Morris earned a B.S. degree in Business Administration from the University of North Alabama and an M.S. in Urban Affairs (with honors) from Alabama A & M University. Mr. Morris is Accountability Specialist for the Memphis City Schools System (MCS), the largest public school system in Tennessee and the nation's 21st largest school district. His responsibilities include strategic planning facilitation and the coordination of school accreditation activities for the district's 175 Schools. Prior to joining MCS in 1995, Mr. Morris held a variety of executive positions in Tennessee, New Jersey, Pennsylvania, and Alabama. Mr. Morris is the co-author of two books, one book chapter, and two journal articles on educating African American children.

DATE DUE

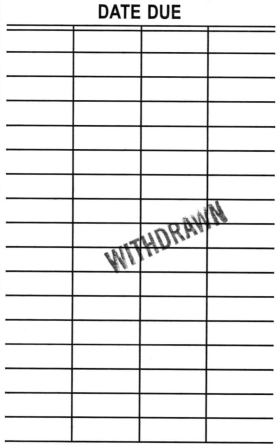

DEMCO 38-296